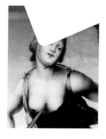

Beccafumi

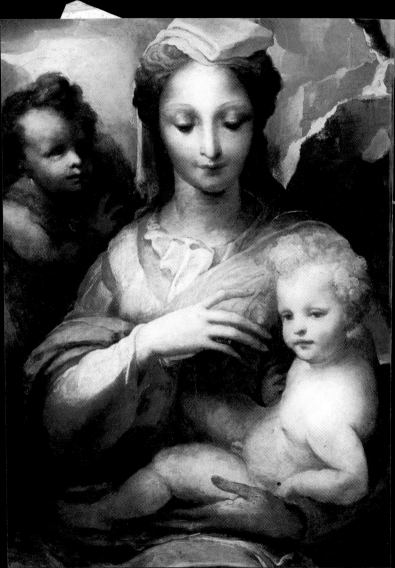

THE LIFE OF

BECCAFUMI

GIORGIO
VASARI

with an introduction by
JENNIFER SLIWKA

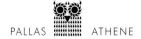

PALLAS ATHENE

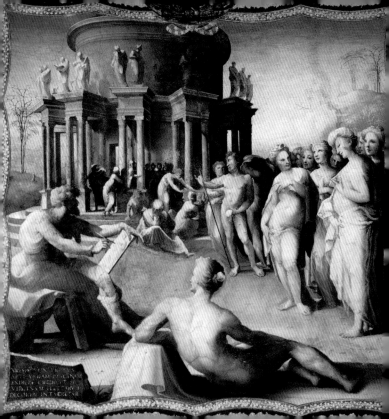

INTRODUCTION

JENNIFER SLIWKA

Frustrated with the lack of perfection he perceived in an altarpiece he was painting in Pisa, Domenico Beccafumi (1484-1551) confessed to Giorgio Vasari that he felt unable to do anything 'away from the air of Siena' and resolved to return to his native city and never again to work elsewhere. This anecdote suggests the degree to which Beccafumi saw the atmosphere and artistic tradition of Siena as vital to his personal and professional success. The rarity of Domenico's excursions beyond the city explains both the scarcity of his works outside the area and, to some extent, why he remains such an enigmatic figure in the history of art. Indeed, despite his prolific career as a painter of altarpieces, frescoes, furniture and illuminated manuscripts, as a printmaker and designer of marble inlay and as a sculptor in wood, bronze and stucco, Beccafumi is rarely discussed in texts on Italian art of this period. Domenico's relative obscurity is all the more surprising considering Vasari's high praise of his works in the 1568 edition of the Lives of the Most Excellent Painters,

Opposite: Zeuxis and the Young Women of Croton, 1519

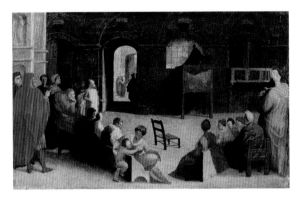

Sienese saints: St. Bernardino preaching, 1535-37

Sculptors and Architects, *an honour the biographer normally reserved for artists working in his beloved Florence.*

The Lives *consists of biographies of all of the major artists of the previous three hundred years, with an overall thesis that the visual arts underwent a period of sustained improvement over the centuries, culminating in with the achievements of Michelangelo. Vasari's* Life of Beccafumi *is particularly important for our understanding of the artist as, aside from limited archival documents, it is essentially the sole source of information for this very private man whom the biographer describes as 'virtuous, God-fearing and extremely solitary'.*

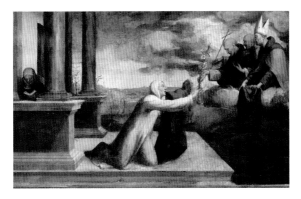

St. Catherine receiving the habit of the Order of St. Dominic, 1514-15

Vasari's history of art opens with the pioneering work of Cimabue and Giotto and concludes with the apotheosis of the 'divine' Michelangelo. Essentially mythologizing Beccafumi's artistic beginnings, Vasari introduces Domenico's life by likening his natural skill to that of Giotto. As in his biography of the Florentine Trecento artist, Vasari recounts how, as a boy, Domenico di Pace (the artist's birth name) would pass the time by drawing on rocks and with a stick in the sand while minding his father's sheep, until, one day, his talent was noticed by Lorenzo Beccafumi who was passing by. Lorenzo convinced Domenico's father to allow him to take the boy to *the city to apprentice in a painter's workshop and eventually bestowed his surname upon the young artist. Though Vasari knew Domenico personally and even collected his drawings and prints, parts of the account of his artistic origins are almost certainly fictionalized in order to place him, like Giotto, at the head of a new artistic tradition, as a similarly important innovator and creative force.*

While the details of the artist's early career remain largely speculative, it is very likely that Beccafumi joined his contemporaries in sketching from the works of the fourteenth and fifteenth century masters of the so-called Sienese Golden Age including Duccio, Simone Martini and the Lorenzetti brothers. Beccafumi's devotion to this tradition is visible in his works, which recall the 'Gothic' sway of the trecento sculptures from the façade of Siena Cathedral, the soft folds of Duccio's draperies and the sinuous lines of Simone's figures. In reworking compositions and leitmotifs from the 'golden age' of Sienese painting, Beccafumi continued an artistic tradition which, over the centuries, had developed into a distinct visual language, a marker of Sienese civic identity.

With the arrival of a number of foreign artists to the city in the late fifteenth and sixteenth centuries, Sienese artists working in this self-referential style slowly began to incorporate elements of these new models and techniques into their works. According to Vasari, Perugino, who by

1502 was working for the Chigi family in the Sienese church of Sant'Agostino, particularly inspired the young Domenico who made sketches after his works. Native and foreign artists alike flocked to Siena Cathedral which essentially became a training ground for young artists to study and imitate the works of their predecessors. The young Raphael, for example, arrived in Siena to work as an assistant to Pinturicchio on the decoration of the Piccolomini Library in the Cathedral whilst Michelangelo was creating some of his earliest sculptures for the Piccolomini altar nearby. It was perhaps the work of Giovan'Antonio Bazzi, known as 'Il Sodoma', however, which most inspired Beccafumi. The Piedmontese artist arrived in Siena in the first years of the century via Milan where he had absorbed the expressive potential of Leonardo's sfumato technique. These softly blended tonal gradations and effects of light and shadow so captured Domenico's imagination that he rapidly adopted them and made them his own. As a result, he soon became one of Sodoma's strongest rivals for the city's most prestigious commissions.

Few of Beccafumi's works have been dated to the period preceding his first trip to Rome around 1510-12. However, one can discern a stylistic shift in his art after this time, which combines the lessons of his native tradition with those of the Roman works of Michelangelo and

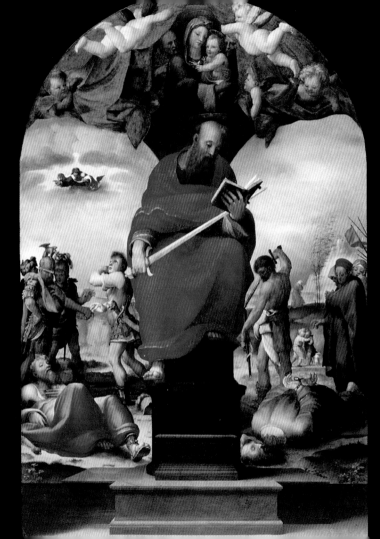

Raphael. New to the papal city, Beccafumi probably joined the circle of more established Sienese citizens residing there such as Agostino Chigi, Pope Julius II's banker, and Baldassare Peruzzi, the painter and architect working on Chigi's villa (now Villa Farnesina) alongside Raphael and his workshop. Vasari recounts how Beccafumi closely studied ancient sculptures and Raphael's Vatican Stanze, though it was certainly the muscular torsos and exaggerated contortions of Michelangelo's Sistine ceiling that left a lasting impression on the young artist. Beccafumi continued to cite and reinterpret these figures in his own works throughout his career, suggesting that despite being 'away from the air of Siena,' this was a particularly profitable time for the artist.

Vasari attributes Domenico's increasingly bold draughtsmanship and prolific inventions to the his Roman sojourn. Beccafumi's whimsical approach, described by the biographer as 'capricciosissimo,' is visible for example in his inclusion of playful anecdotal details: the nude child reclining coquettishly on the steps during the solemn rites of the Ceralia (formerly known as the Vestalia, Florence, Museo di Casa Martelli), the ubiquitous little white dog, who runs from a stick-wielding

Opposite: St Paul Enthroned, 1516-17

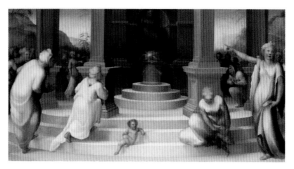

The Cult of Ceres (Ceralia), 1519

putto along an initial 'L' in an illuminated manuscript (Florence, Uffizi) or bites at the ankle of the little boy in the Betrothal of the Virgin *(Siena, Oratorio di San Bernardino). There is also a strong element of* fantasia, *or imagination, in the artist's work, epitomized by the first version of the* Saint Michael casting out the rebel angels *for the Church of the Carmine (Siena, Pinacoteca Nazionale; see p. 39). In this panel, an innovatively fore-shortened God the Father soars over the archangel Michael whose magnificent peacock wings span the upper register of the panel, while the rebel angels with butterfly wings and clawed feet swoop and dive acrobatically below.*

Returning to Siena from Rome, one of Domenico's first

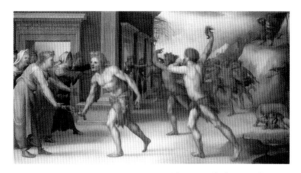

The Festival of Lupercalia, 1519

commissions was the decoration of the façade of Palazzo Borghesi in an elite neighbourhood of the city. In accepting this job, Beccafumi effectively entered into a high profile competition with Sodoma, who at the time was adorning the façade of Palazzo Bardi facing the Borghesi palace across the Piazza di Postierla. The original appearance of Beccafumi's now lost decoration can be reconstructed through a sketch (London, The British Museum; see p. 30) which illustrates a façade animated by battle scenes and gods and heroes from Roman history painted in chiaroscuro in imitation of antique statuary. This early work, which may have inspired Prince Doria to hire Beccafumi to decorate his palace in Genoa decades later, introduces themes and techniques that Domenico

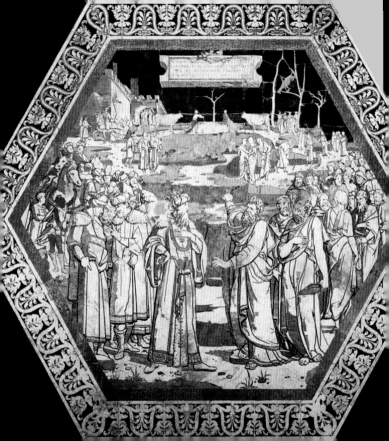

continued to employ and develop, in increasingly sophisticated forms, throughout his career. For example, the somewhat oblique classical references on the façade are superseded by the erudite scenes from ancient history in the iconographically complex fresco cycles in the vaults of the Palazzo Venturi and the Sala del Concistoro in the Palazzo Pubblico from the 1520s and 30s respectively. The chiaroscuro façade also presented Beccafumi with a series of artistic problems regarding the role of light and shadow in the creation of form which he continued to address, in a variety of different media, over the rest of his career. It was undoubtedly his designs for the marble inlay floors of Siena Cathedral however, which most fully exploited the technique. This commission, described by Vasari as: 'a school and pastime for Domenico which he never fully gave up in favour of other work' occupied almost three decades of the artist's life from about 1519-47. After creating life-size cartoons which served as guides for the stonecutters, Beccafumi painted over them with varying shades of ochre-grey wash to indicate where areas of darker marble should be inserted into the sections of lighter stone. The effect of the floor can be likened to an enormous jigsaw puzzle of marble figures which were then articulated through a sgraffito, literally 'scratched-in', technique of

Opposite: Elijah and Ahab, marble inlay floor in Siena Cathedral, c. 1524

modelling. Though the process of paving the Cathedral using marble inlay was begun centuries earlier, Beccafumi's innovative intarsia designs, executed to an unsurpassed level of high finish, truly evoke the 'paintings in stone' praised by Vasari.

In this same period, Domenico began producing monochrome oil sketches on paper – an unprecedented technique which was not mastered to the same degree until the seventeenth century. The technique proved to be an ideal vehicle for Beccafumi's invention and experimentation owing to the fluidity of the oil medium and its dramatic chiaroscuro effects. In the 1540s Domenico transferred the knowledge he had gleaned from these oil studies into another medium: chiaroscuro woodblock prints, for which he carved multiple (generally three) blocks, each painted with a different shade of ink and superimposed on the sheet.

The artist's concern for light effects was not restricted to his experimentations in monochrome however, and they are exploited to a different end in works such as the Nativity *of the 1520s (Siena, San Martino; see p. 35) in which a diffuse, penumbral glow contributes to the spiritual or otherworldly quality of the scene. Beccafumi is perhaps known better still for his* colorito, *or application*

Opposite: Study of old man, oil on paper, c. 1524

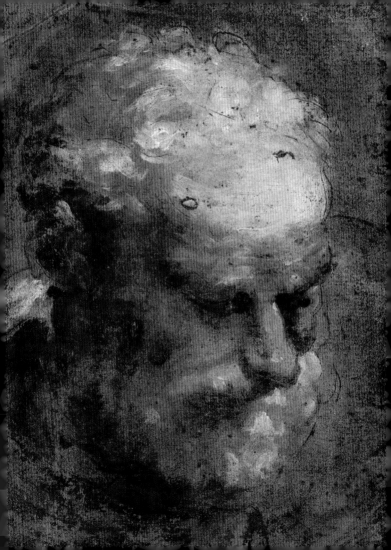

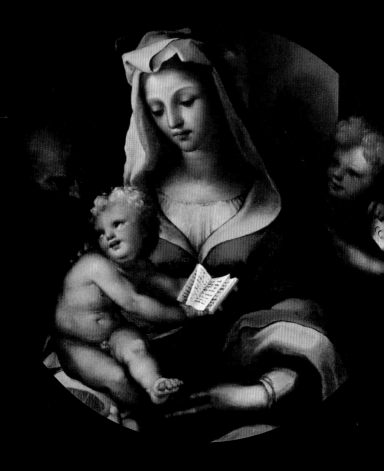

of colour, in works such as his Venus and Cupid *(Birmingham, Barber Institute of Fine Arts) and the* Virgin and Child with St. Jerome and the Infant St. John *tondo (Madrid, Museo Thyssen-Bornemisza) in which brilliant yellows are juxtaposed with salmon pinks and acidic greens stand out against deep purple-blues. As in his chiaroscuro works, the highlights here contrast starkly with the dark backgrounds, so that the figures emanate an almost phosphorescent glow and acquire a supernatural quality which recalls the visionary aspect of early Sienese art.*

Beccafumi's late paintings however tend towards a more muted colour palette, visible for example in the St. Catherine *dating to the mid 1540s, (Rotterdam, Boymans-van Beuningen Museum; see p. 21) while his drawings acquire a looser, more 'impressionistic' style. Similarly, the bold linearism of his early pavements contrasts with the 'sketchy', almost ethereal quality of his later floors. Beccafumi became increasingly devoted to sculpture towards the end of his life, notably in his bronze angels for the Cathedral, and embraced a more 'stripped-down' aesthetic. This shift suggests a more decorous or pious sensibility in the 'God-fearing' artist during the final years of*

Opposite: Virgin and Child with St. Jerome and the Infant St. John, c. 1519

his life and perhaps also an awareness of the increasing anxieties regarding religious images addressed at the Council of Trent.

It was during the long, solitary and laborious process of casting the bronze angels for Siena Cathedral that Beccafumi succumbed to his death in 1551. According to Vasari, Beccafumi's body was subsequently carried in procession by all of the artisans in the city to his tomb in the Duomo where he was eulogized with an honour befitting his talent and virtue. Though Vasari confuses the year of Beccafumi's demise, his account is in keeping with contemporary funereal rites of important artistic figures and is most likely accurate. The praises that rang out from the Cathedral that day, echoed by Vasari, were repeated in subsequent years by Sienese chroniclers such as Fabio Chigi and by foreign authors including Felipe de Guevara. These accounts encouraged the collection of Beccafumi's works by esteemed figures, including the seventeenth century Medici Grand-Dukes who were 'taste-makers' in their own right. While appreciation for Beccafumi's work continued through the eighteenth century, as Guglielmo Della Valle's Lettere Sanesi *suggest, there was an increasing value placed upon classicizing works, exemplified by the author's preference for the*

Opposite: St. Catherine receiving the Stigmata, c. 1545

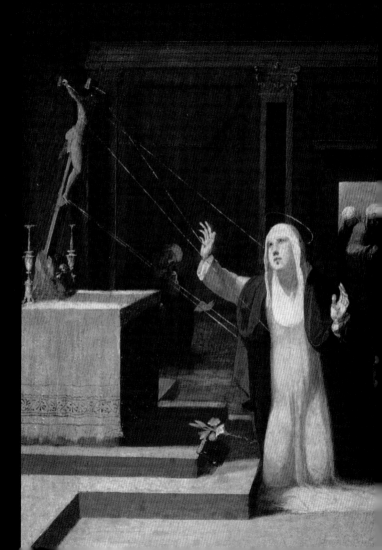

vault frescoes of Palazzo Venturi over Beccafumi's more innovative and capricious works.

Domenico's critical fortune changed considerably with the more decorous taste of the nineteenth century, a period disinterested in the 'perversions' of Maniera painting with its purportedly gratuitous inclusions of contorted bodies, unnatural colours and affected 'manner'. Indeed, Beccafumi's name is often invoked in discussions of Florentine artists of the Maniera such as Jacopo Pontormo and Rosso Fiorentino, and the reception of his work appears to have suffered alongside theirs. Nineteenth century indifference developed into distaste for the style in the early twentieth century. Langton Douglas, for example, launches into a full attack of Beccafumi's 'skimble-skamble' achievements, describing the artist as having 'little sense of artistic fitness' and scorning his 'ludicrous attempts' at rendering chiaroscuro with inlaid marbles. Analogously, Walter Friedländer, who first applied the term 'Mannerism' to the painting of this period, dismissed the style as 'anti-classical' and favoured instead the normative ideals of the High Renaissance epitomized by the beautiful and harmonious style of Raphael. Subsequent scholars continued to characterize the art of the Maniera in fairly negative terms, describing it variously as formulaic, courtly, academic, decadent, fantastical, macabre or angst-ridden.

Fortunately, post-war art criticism seemed to embrace a re-evaluation of the writings of earlier critics, leading to a shift in the perception of these works which is reflected in the increasing number of publications and exhibitions dedicated to the Maniera and in the more nuanced appreciation for the various aims and aspirations of the style. This reconsideration of both the art and of the term 'Maniera' itself allowed for a more objective view of Beccafumi's artistic accomplishments, such as his ability to embrace this new aesthetic while remaining rooted in the Sienese artistic tradition. Scholars have often disparagingly described the Sienese practice of reworking compositions and motifs from their 'Golden Age' as 'conservative' and lacking in artistic imagination. More recently however, it has been demonstrated that there was a decidedly political and patriotic dimension to this reiteration through which the Sienese reinforced their civic identity and independence – particularly from Florence, their long-standing enemy.

Perhaps unsurprisingly therefore, Beccafumi distanced himself from contemporary artistic developments in Florence in favour of the lessons of Rome – a city with which Siena had an enduring affinity. In adopting a Roman artistic language, an alternative to the popular Florentine idiom, and incorporating it into his own native tradition, Beccafumi created a more personal interpretation of the Italian Maniera. In participating in the decoration of the primary private, civic and religious sites of the city however, one may argue that Beccafumi's signature style soon became a synecdoche for the ideals of the Republic as a whole. Finally, in a curious twist of fate, shortly after the death of this 'official painter of the Sienese Republic', the city capitulated to the Hapsburg Emperor Charles V and his Florentine allies and, after centuries of rivalry between the two cities, Siena's status as an independent republic was irretrievably lost.

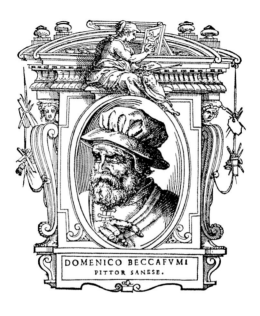

DOMENICO BECCAFVMI
PITTOR SANESE.

The Life of Domenico Beccafumi
Painter and Master of Casting
of Siena

GIORGIO VASARI

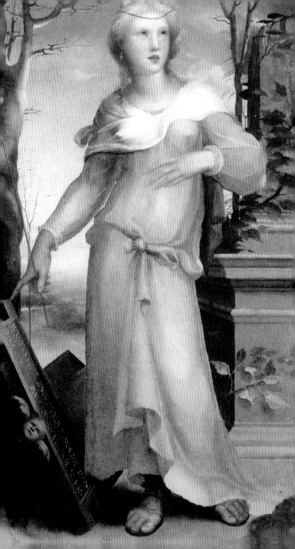

THAT same quality, the pure gift of nature, which has been seen in Giotto and in some others among those painters of whom we have spoken hitherto, has been revealed most recently in Domenico Beccafumi, the painter of Siena, in that he, while guarding some sheep for his father Pacio, the labourer of the Sienese citizen Lorenzo Beccafumi, was observed to practise his hand by himself, child as he was, in drawing sometimes on stones and sometimes in other ways. It happened that the said Lorenzo saw him one day drawing various things with a pointed stick on the sand of a small stream, where he was watching his little charges, and he asked for the child from his father, meaning to employ him as his servant, and at the same time to have him taught. The boy, therefore, who was then called Mecherino, having been given up by his father Pacio to Lorenzo, was taken to Siena, where Lorenzo caused him for a while to spend all the spare time that he had after his household duties in the workshop of a painter who was his neighbour. This painter, who was no great craftsman, caused Mecherino to learn all that he could not himself teach him from drawings by eminent

Opposite: Tanaquil, c. 1519

painters that he had in his possession, of which he
availed himself for his own purposes, as those masters are wont to do who are not very able in drawing. Exercising his hand, therefore, in this manner,
Mecherino gave promise of being destined to
become an excellent painter.

During this time Pietro Perugino, then a famous
painter, came to Siena, where, as has been related,
he painted two altarpieces; and his manner pleased
Domenico greatly, so that he set himself to study it
and to copy those altar-pieces, and no long time
passed before he had caught that manner. Then,
after Michelangelo's Chapel and the works of
Raphael had been thrown open in Rome,
Domenico, who desired nothing so much as to learn,
and knew that he was wasting his time in Siena, took
leave of Lorenzo Beccafumi, from whom he
acquired the family name of Beccafumi, and made
his way to Rome. There he placed himself under a
painter, who gave him board and lodging, and executed many works in company with him, giving his
attention at the same time to studying the works of
Michelangelo, Raphael, and other eminent masters,
and the marvellous statues and sarcophagi of anti-
quity. No long time passed, therefore, before he
became a bold draughtsman, fertile in invention,

and a very pleasing colourist; but during this period, which did not exceed two years, he did nothing worthy of record save a façade in the Borgo with an escutcheon of Pope Julius II in colour.[1]

Meanwhile, there had been brought to Siena by a merchant of the Spannocchi family, as will be related in the proper place, the painter Giovanni Antonio of Vercelli, a young man of passing good ability, who was much employed, particularly in making portraits from life, by the gentlemen of that city, which has always been the friend and patron of all men of talent. Domenico, who was very desirous of returning to his own country, having heard this news, made his way back to Siena; and when he saw that Giovanni Antonio was very well grounded in drawing, which he knew to be the essence of the excellence of a craftsman, not resting content with what he had done in Rome, he set himself with the utmost zeal to follow him, devoting himself much to anatomy and to drawing nudes; which helped him so much, that in a short time he began to be greatly esteemed in that most noble city. Nor was he beloved less for his goodness and his character than for his art, for the reason that, whereas Giovanni Antonio

[1] No longer survives.

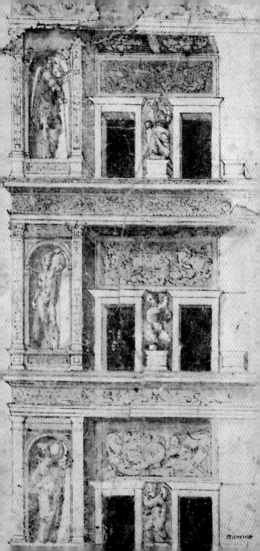

was coarse, licentious, and eccentric, being called Il Sodoma because he always mixed and lived with beardless boys, and answering willingly enough to that name, Domenico, on the other hand, was a pattern of good conduct and uprightness, living like a Christian and keeping very much to himself. But such persons as are called merry fellows and good companions are very often more esteemed by men than the virtuous and orderly, and most of the young men of Siena followed Sodoma, extolling him as a man of originality. And this Sodoma, being an eccentric, and wishing to please the common herd, always kept at his house parrots, apes, dwarf donkeys, little Elba horses, a talking raven, Barb horses for running races, and other suchlike creatures; from which he had won such a name among the vulgar, that they spoke of nothing but his follies.

Sodoma, then, had painted with colours in fresco the façade of the house of M. Agostino Bardi, and Domenico at the same time, in competition with him, painted the façade of a house of the Borghesi, close to the Postierla column, near the Duomo, over which he took very great pains.[1] Below the roof, in a

[1.] No longer survives, but known from a preparatory drawing

Opposite: Sketch for a façade decoration for the Borghesi, c. 1512

frieze in chiaroscuro, he executed some little figures
that were much praised; and in the spaces between
the three ranges of windows of travertine that adorn
that palace, he painted many ancient gods and other
figures in imitation of bronze, in chiaroscuro and in
colour, which were more than passing good,
although the work of Sodoma was more highly
praised. Both these façades were executed in the
year 1512.

Domenico afterwards painted for S. Benedetto,
a seat of Monks of Monte Oliveto, outside the Porta
Tufi, an altarpiece of St Catharine of Siena in a
building receiving the Stigmata, with a St Benedict
standing on her right hand, and on her left a St
Jerome in the habit of a Cardinal; which altarpiece,
being very soft in colouring and strong in relief, was
much praised, as it still is.[1] In the predella of this picture, likewise, he painted some little scenes in tempera with incredible boldness and vivacity, and with
such facility of design, that they could not be more
graceful, and yet they have the appearance of having been executed without the slightest effort in the

[1] Pinacoteca Nazionale, Siena

*Opposite: St Catharine receiving the Stigmata, 1514-1515.
One of the predella scenes is reproduced p. 7*

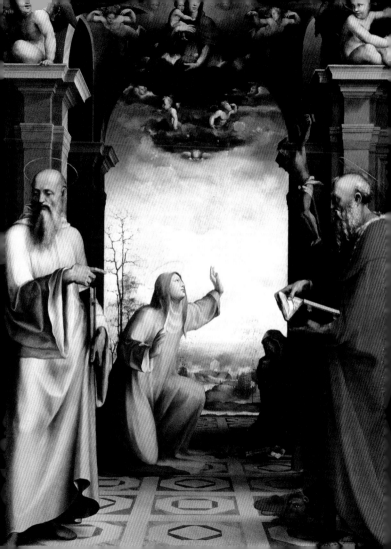

world. In one of these little scenes is the Angel placing in the mouth of that same St Catharine part of the Host consecrated by the priest; in another Jesus Christ is marrying her, in a third she is receiving the habit from St Dominic, and there are other stories.

For the Church of S. Martino the same master painted a large altarpiece with Christ born and being adored by the Virgin, by Joseph, and by the Shepherds; and above the hut is a most beautiful choir of Angels dancing.[1] In this work, which is much praised by artists, Domenico began to show to those who had some understanding that his works were painted with a different foundation from those of Sodoma. He then painted in fresco, in the Great Hospital, the Madonna visiting St Elizabeth, in a manner very pleasing and very natural.[2] And for the Church of S. Spirito he executed an altarpiece of the Madonna holding in her arms the Child, who is marrying the above-mentioned St Catharine of Siena, and at the sides St Bernardino, St Francis, St Jerome, and St Catharine the Virgin-Martyr, with St Peter and St Paul upon some marble steps in front, on the polished surface of which he counterfeited

[1] Still in situ [2] Still in situ

Opposite: The Nativity, c. 1522

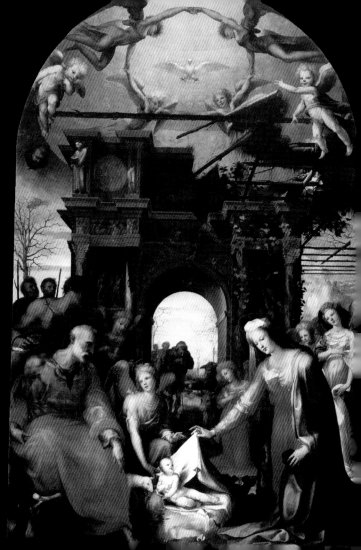

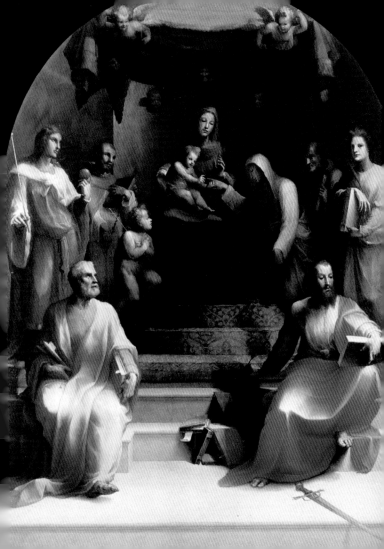

with great art some reflections of the colour of their draperies.[1] This work, which was executed with fine judgment and design, brought him much honour, as did also some little figures painted on the predella of the picture, in which is St John baptizing Christ,[2] a King causing the wife and children of St Sigismund to be thrown into a well,[3] St Dominic burning the books of the heretics,[4] Christ presenting to St Catharine of Siena two crowns, one of roses and the other of thorns,[5] and St Bernardino of Siena preaching on the Piazza of Siena to a vast multitude.[6]

Next, by reason of the fame of these works, there was allotted to Domenico an altarpiece that was to be placed in the Carmine, in which he had to paint a St Michael wreaking vengeance on Lucifer; and he, being full of fancy, set himself to think out a new invention, in order to display his talent and the beautiful conceptions of his brain. And so, seeking to represent Lucifer and his followers driven for their

[1] Siena, Monte de' Paschi di Siena, Chigi-Saracini collection. Predella removed before 1786   [2] & [5] Philbrook Art Centre, Tulsa, Oklahoma   [3] & [4] Known from copies now in Museum of Fine Arts, Boston   [6] Private collection, London

Opposite: Mystic Marriage of St. Catherine with Saints, 1528

pride from Heaven to the lowest depths of Hell, he began a shower of nude figures raining down, which is very beautiful, although, from his having taken too great pains with it, it appears if anything rather confused.[1] This altarpiece, which remained unfinished, was taken after the death of Domenico to the Great Hospital and placed at the top of some steps near the high altar, where it is still regarded with marvel on account of some very beautiful foreshortenings in the nudes. In the Carmine, where this picture was to have been set up, was placed another, in the upper part of which is represented a God the Father above the clouds with many Angels round Him, painted with marvellous grace; and in the centre of the picture is the Angel Michael in armour, flying, and pointing to Lucifer, whom he has driven to the centre of the earth, where there are burning buildings, rugged caverns, and a lake of fire, with Angels in various attitudes, and nude figures of lost souls, who are swimming with different gestures of agony in that fire.[2] All this is painted with such beauty and grace of manner, that it appears that this marvellous

[1] Siena, Pinacoteca Nazionale   [2] Still in situ

Opposite: St Michael Driving out the Rebel Angels, 1524

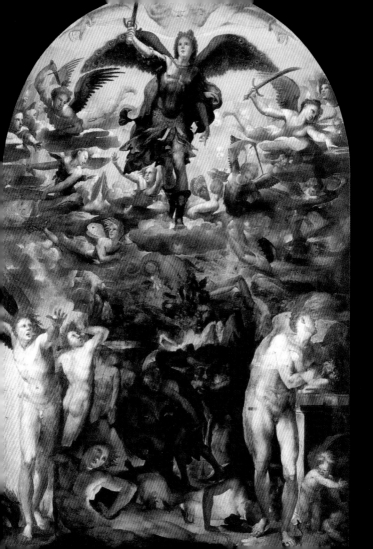

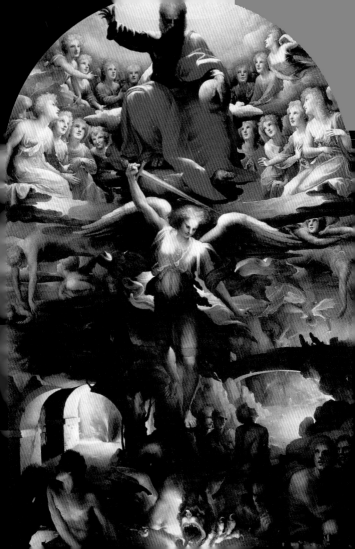

work, in its thick darkness, is illuminated by the fire; wherefore it is held to be a rare picture. Baldassarre Peruzzi of Siena, an excellent painter, could never have his fill of praising it, and I myself, one day that I saw it uncovered in his company, while passing through Siena, was struck with astonishment by it, as I also was by the five little scenes that are in the predella, painted with tempera in a judicious and beautiful manner.[1] For the Nuns of Ognissanti in the same city Domenico painted another altarpiece, in which is Christ on high in the heavens, crowning the Glorified Virgin, and below them are St Gregory, St Anthony, St Mary Magdalene, and St Catharine the Virgin-Martyr; and in the predella, likewise, are some very beautiful little figures executed in tempera.[2]

In the house of Signor Marcello Agostini Domenico[3] painted some very lovely works in fresco on the ceiling of an apartment, which has three lunettes on each main side and two at each end, with

[1] Predella removed in 1688; two scenes survive in the Carnegie Museum of Art, Pittsburgh   [2] Altarpiece Siena, church of S. Spirito; predella panels in private collection   [3] Now Palazzo Bindi-Sergardi

Opposite: St Michael Driving out the Rebel Angels, 1528

a series of friezes that go right round. The centre of the ceiling is divided into two quadrangular compartments; in the first, where a silken arras is counterfeited as upheld by the ornament, there may be seen, as if woven upon it, Scipio Africanus restoring the young woman untouched to her husband, and in the other the celebrated painter Zeuxis, who is drawing several nude women in order to paint his picture, which was to be placed in the Temple of Juno.* In one of the lunettes, painted with little figures only about half a braccio high, but very beautiful, are the two Roman brothers who, having been enemies, became friends for the public good and for the sake of their country.† In that which follows is Torquatus, who, in order to observe the laws, when his son has been condemned to lose his eyes, causes one of his son's and one of his own to be put out.‡ In the next is the Petition of...,§ who, after hearing the recital of his crimes against his country and the Roman people, is put to death. In the lunette beside that one is the Roman people deliberating on the

* See p. 4 †In fact Oath of Attilius Regulus ‡In fact Zeleucos of Locris § There is an omission in the text here. The subject is the Execution of Spurius Cassius

Opposite: The Continence of Scipio, 1519

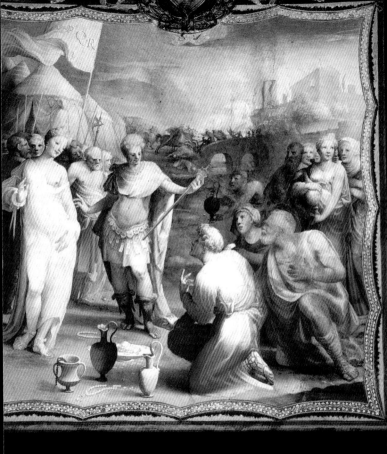

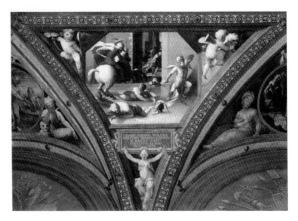

Death of Cato of Utica, 1519

expedition of Scipio to Africa; and next to this, in another lunette, is an ancient sacrifice crowded with a variety of most beautiful figures, with a temple drawn in perspective, which has no little relief, for in that field Domenico was a truly excellent master. In the last is Cato killing himself after being overtaken by some horsemen that are most beautifully painted there. And in the recesses of the lunettes, also, are some little scenes very well finished.

The excellence of this work was the reason that Domenico was recognized as a rare painter by those who were then governing, and was commissioned to paint the vaulting of a hall in the Palace of the Signori, to which he devoted all the diligence, study, and effort of which any man is capable, in order to prove his worth and to adorn that celebrated building of his native city, which was honouring him so much. This hall,* which is two squares long and one square wide, has the ceiling made not with lunettes, but after the manner of a groined vaulting; wherefore Domenico executed the compartments in painting, thinking that this would give the best result, with friezes and cornices overlaid with gold, and all so beautifully, that, without any stucco-work or other ornaments, they are so well painted and so graceful that they appear to be really in relief. On each of the two ends of this hall there is a large picture with an historical scene, and on each main wall there are two, one on either side of an octagon; and thus the pictures are six and the octagons two, and in each of the latter is a scene. At each corner of the vaulting, where the rib is, there is drawn a round compartment, which extends half on one wall and half on the other, so that these compartments, being divided by the ribs of the vaulting, form eight spaces, in each

* Sala di Concistoro of the Palazzo Pubblico, Siena

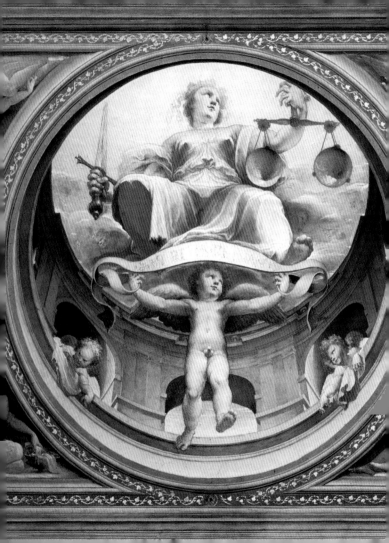

of which are large seated figures, representing distinguished men who have defended their Republic and have observed her laws. The highest part of the surface of the vaulting is divided into three parts, in such a manner as to form a circular compartment in the centre, immediately above the octagons, and two square compartments over those on the walls.

In one of the octagons, then, is a woman with some children round her, who holds a heart in her hand, representing the love that men owe to their country. In the other octagon is another woman, with an equal number of children, as a symbol of civic concord. And these are one on either side of a Justice that is in the circle, with the sword and scales in her hands, and seen from below in such bold foreshortening that it is a marvel, for at the feet she is dark both in drawing and in colour, and about the knees she becomes lighter, and so continues little by little towards the torso, the shoulders, and the arms, until she rises into a celestial splendour at the head, which makes it appear as if that figure dissolves gradually in a mist: wherefore it is not possible to imagine, much less to see, a more beautiful figure than this one, or one executed with greater judgment

Opposite: Justice, 1529-35

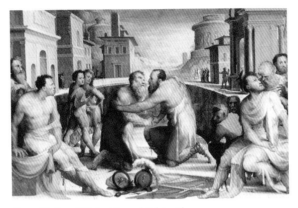

Reconciliation of M. Lepidus and Fulvius Flaccus, 1529-35

and art, among all that were ever painted to be seen in foreshortening from below.

As for the stories, in the first, at the end of the hall and on the left hand as one enters, are M. Lepidus and Fulvius Flaccus the Censors, who, after being at enmity with one another, as soon as they became colleagues in the office of the Censorship, laid aside their private hatred for the good of their country, and acted in that office like the closest friends. And Domenico painted them on their knees, embracing each other, with many figures round

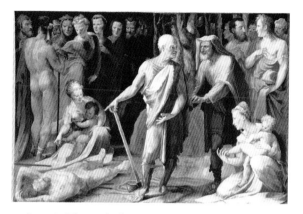

Postumius Tiburtius has his son executed for insubordination, 1529-35

them, and with a most beautiful prospect of buildings and temples drawn in perspective so ingeniously and so well, that one may see in them what a master of perspective was Domenico. On the next wall there follows a picture with the story of the Dictator Postumius Tiburtius, who, having left his only son at the head of his army in place of himself, commanding him that he should do nothing else but guard the camp, put him to death for having been disobedient and having with a fair occasion attacked the enemy and gained a victory. In this scene Domenico painted

49

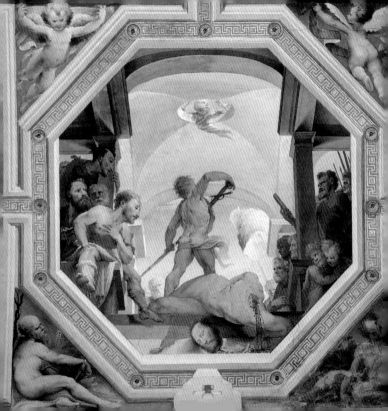

Postumius as an old man with shaven face, with the right hand on his axe, and with the left showing to the army his son lying dead upon the ground, and depicted very well in foreshortening; and below this picture, which is most beautiful, is an inscription very well composed. In the octagon that follows, in the centre of the wall, is the story of Spurius Cassius, whom the Roman Senate, suspecting that he was plotting to become King, caused to be beheaded, and his house to be pulled down; and in this scene the head, which is beside the executioner, and the body, which is on the ground in fore-shortening, are very beautiful. In the next picture is the Tribune Publius Mucius, who caused all his fel-low-tribunes, who were conspiring with Spurius to become tyrants of their country, to be burned; and here the fire that is consuming their bodies is paint-ed very well and with great art.

At the other end of the hall, in another picture, is the Athenian Codrus, who, having heard from the oracle that the victory would fall to that side whose King should be killed by the enemy, laid aside his robes, entered unknown among the enemy, and let himself be slain, thus giving the victory to his people

Opposite: Execution of Spurius Cassius, 1529-35

by his own death. Domenico painted him seated, with his nobles round him as he puts off his robes, near a most beautiful round temple; and in the distant background of the picture he is seen dead, with his name in an epitaph below. Then, as one turns to the other long wall, opposite to the two pictures with the octagon in the centre between them, in the first scene one finds Prince Zaleucus, who, in order not to break the law, caused one of his own eyes to be put out, and one of his son's; and here many are standing round him, praying him that he should not do that cruelty to himself and his son, and in the distance is his son offering violence to a maiden, and below is his name in an inscription. In the octagon that is beside that picture is the story of Marcus Manilius being hurled down from the Capitol; and the figure of the young Marcus, who is being thrown down from a kind of balcony, is painted so well in foreshortening, with the head downwards, that it seems to be alive, as also seem some figures that are below. In the next picture is Spurius Melius, who belonged to the Equestrian Order, and was killed by the Tribune Servilius because the people suspected that he was conspiring to become tyrant of his

Opposite: Marcus Manilius being thrown to his death, 1529-35

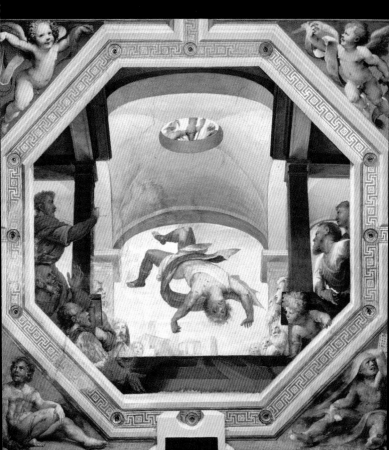

country; which Servilius is seated with many round him, and one who is in the centre points to Spurius lying dead upon the ground, a figure painted with great art.

Then, in the circles at the corners, where there are the eight figures mentioned above, are many men who have been distinguished for their defence of their country. In the first part is the famous Fabius Maximus, seated and in armour; and on the other side is Speusippus, Prince of the Tegeatæ, who, being exhorted by a friend that he should rid himself of his rival and adversary, answered that he did not wish, at the bidding of his own private interest, to deprive his country of such a citizen. In the circle that is at the next corner, in one part, there is the Prætor Celius, who, for having fought against the advice and wish of the soothsayers, although he had won and had gained a victory, was punished by the Senate; and beside him sits Thrasybulus, who with the aid of some friends valorously slew thirty tyrants, in order to free his country. Thrasybulus is an old man, shaven, with white locks, and has his name written beneath him, as have also all the others. In a circle at one corner of the lower end of the hall is the Prætor Genutius Cippus, who having had a bird with wings in the form of horns miraculously alight on his head, was told by the oracle that he would become King of his country, whereupon, although already an old man, he chose to go into exile, in order not to take away her liberty; and Domenico therefore painted a bird upon his head. Beside him sits Charondas, who, having returned from the country, and having gone straightway into the Senate without disarming himself, in violation of a law which ordained that one who entered the Senate with arms should be put to death, killed himself on perceiving his error. In the second circle on the other side are Damon and Phintias, whose unexampled friendship is so well known, and with them is Dionysius, Tyrant of Sicily; and beside these figures sits Brutus, who from love of his country condemned his two sons to death, because they were conspiring to bring the Tarquins back to their country.

This work, then, so truly extraordinary, made known to the people of Siena the ability and worth of Domenico, who showed most beautiful art, judgment, and genius in all that he did.

The first time that the Emperor Charles V came to Italy, it was expected that he would go to Siena, for he had declared such an intention to the Ambassadors of that Republic; and among other vast and magnificent preparations that were made for the reception of so great an Emperor, Domenico fashioned a horse eight braccia high and in full relief, all of paste-board and hollow within. The weight of that horse was supported by an armature of iron, and upon it was the statue of the Emperor, armed in the ancient fashion, with a sword in his hand. And below it were three large figures – vanquished by him, as it were – which also supported part of the weight, the horse being in the act of leaping with the front legs high in the air; which three figures represented three provinces conquered and subdued by the Emperor.* In that work Domenico showed that he was a master no less of sculpture than of painting; to which it must be added that he had placed the whole work upon a wooden structure four braccia high, with a number of wheels below it, which, being set in motion by men concealed within, caused the whole to move forward; and the design of Domenico was that at the entry of His Majesty this horse, having been set in motion as has been described, should accompany him from the gate as far as the Palace of the Signori, and should then come to rest in the middle of the Piazza. This horse, after being carried by Domenico

* Lost

so near completion that there only remained to gild it, was left in that condition, because His Majesty after all did not at that time go to Siena, but left Italy after being crowned at Bologna; and the work remained unfinished. But none the less the art and ingenuity of Domenico were recognized, and all men greatly praised the grandeur and excellence of that great structure, which stood in the Office of Works of the Duomo from that time until His Majesty, returning from his victorious enterprise in Africa, passed through Messina and then Naples, Rome, and finally Siena; at which time Domenico's work was placed on the Piazza del Duomo, to his great honour.

The fame of the ability of Domenico being thus spread abroad, Prince Doria, who was with the Court, after seeing all the works by his hand that were in Siena, besought him that he should go to Genoa to work in his palace, where Perino del Vaga, Giovanni Antonio da Pordenone, and Girolamo da Treviso had worked. But Domenico could not promise that lord that he would go to serve him at that time, although he engaged himself for another time, for in those days he had set his hand to finishing a part of the marble pavement in the Duomo, which Duccio, the painter of Siena, had formerly begun in a new manner of work. The figures and scenes were already in great part designed on the marble, the outlines being hollowed out with the chisel and filled with a black mixture, with ornaments of coloured marble all around, and likewise the grounds for the figures. But Domenico, with fine judgment, saw that this work could be much improved, and he therefore took grey marbles, to the end that these, profiled with the chisel and placed beside the brilliancy of the white marble, might give the middle shades; and he found that in this way, with white and grey marble, pictures of stone could be made with great perfection after the manner of chiaroscuro. Having then made a trial, the work succeeded so well in invention, in solidity of design, and in abundance of figures, that he made a beginning after this fashion with the grandest, the most beautiful, and the most magnificent pavement that had ever been made; and in the course of his life, little by little, he executed a great part of it.* Round the high altar he made a border of pictures, in which, in order to follow the order of the stories begun by Duccio, he executed scenes from Genesis; namely, Adam and Eve

* The pavement survives, though in variable condition

Opposite: Eve, c. 1544

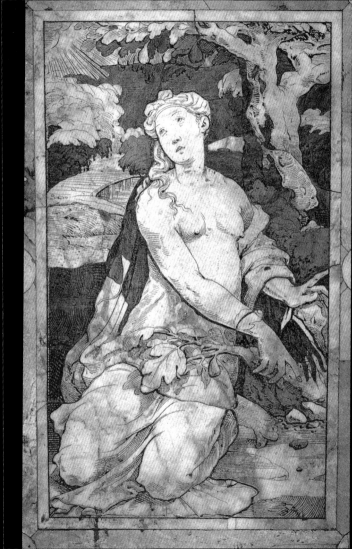

expelled from Paradise and tilling the earth, the Sacrifice of Abel, and that of Melchizedek. In front of the altar is a large scene with Abraham about to sacrifice Isaac, and this has round it a border of half-length figures, carrying various animals which they seem to be going to sacrifice. Descending the steps, one finds another large picture, which serves to accompany that above, and in it Domenico represented Moses receiving the Laws from God on Mount Sinai; and below this is the scene when, having found the people worshipping the Golden Calf, he is seized with anger and breaks the Tables on which those Laws were written. Below this scene, opposite the pulpit, and right across the church, is a frieze with a great number of figures, which is composed with so much grace and such design that it defies description; and in this is Moses, who, striking the rock in the desert, causes water to gush out and gives drink to his thirsty people. Here, along the whole length of the frieze, Domenico represented the stream of water, from which the people are drinking in various ways with a vivacity so pleasing that it is almost impossible to imagine any effect more lovely, or figures in more graceful and beautiful attitudes than are those in this scene – some stooping to the ground to drink, some kneeling before the rock that is spouting with water, some drawing it in vases and others in cups, and others, finally, drinking with their hands. There are, moreover, some who are leading animals to drink, amid the great rejoicing of that people; and, among other things, most marvellous is a little boy who has taken a little dog by the head and neck and plunges its muzzle into the water, in order to make it drink, after which the dog, having drunk, and not wishing to drink any more, shakes its head so naturally that it seems to be alive. In short, this frieze is so beautiful, that for a work of that kind it could not be executed with greater art, seeing that the various kinds of shadows that may be seen in these figures are not merely beautiful, but miraculous; and although the whole work, on account of the fantastic nature of its craftsmanship, is one of great beauty, this part is held to be the most beautiful and the best. Below the cupola, moreover, there is a hexagonal compartment, which is divided into seven hexagons and six rhombs, of which hexagons Domenico finished four before he died, representing in them the stories and sacrifices of Elijah, and doing all this much at his leisure, because this work was as a school and a pastime to Domenico, nor did he ever abandon it altogether for his other works.

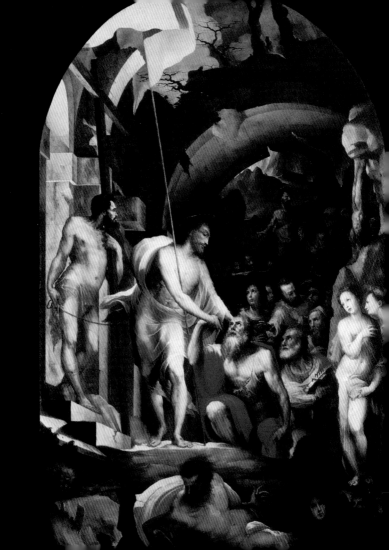

While he was thus labouring now at this work and now elsewhere, he painted a large altar-piece in oils which is in S. Francesco on the right hand as one enters into the church, containing Christ descending in Glory to the Limbo of Hell in order to deliver the Holy Fathers;[1] wherein, among many nudes, is a very beautiful Eve, and a Thief who is behind Christ with the cross is a very well-executed figure, while the cavern of Limbo and the demons and fires of that place are fantastic to a marvel. And since Domenico was of the opinion that pictures painted in tempera preserved their freshness better than those painted in oils, saying that it seemed to him that the works of Luca da Cortona, of the Pollaiuoli, and of the other masters who painted in oils in those days, had suffered from age more than those of Fra Giovanni, Fra Filippo, Benozzo, and the others before their time who painted in tempera – for this reason, I say, having to paint an altarpiece for the Company of S. Bernardino on the Piazza di S. Francesco, he resolved to do it in tempera; and in this way he executed it excellently well, painting in it

[1] Pinacoteca Nazionale, Siena

Opposite: Descent into Limbo, c. 1535

Our Lady with many Saints.[1] In the predella, which is very beautiful, and painted by him likewise in tempera, he depicted St Francis receiving the Stigmata; St Anthony of Padua, who, in order to convert some heretics, performs the miracle of the Ass, which makes obeisance before the sacred Host; and St Bernardino of Siena, who is preaching to the people of his city on the Piazza de' Signori. And on the walls of this Company, also, he painted two stories of Our Lady in fresco, in competition with some others that Sodoma had executed in the same place. In one he represented the Visitation of St Elizabeth, and in the other the Passing of Our Lady, with the Apostles all around; and both of these are much extolled.[2]

Finally, after having been long expected in Genoa by Prince Doria, Domenico made his way there, but with great reluctance, being a man who was accustomed to a life of peace and contented with that which his wants required, and nothing more; besides which, he was not much used to making journeys, for the reason that, having built himself a little house in Siena, and having also a vineyard a

[1] Painted 1535-37 and still in situ; predella panels in Louvre, Paris
[2] Painted 1516-17 and still in situ; the Visitation is in fact the Marriage of the Virgin

mile beyond the Porta Camollia, which he cultivated with his own hands as a recreation, going there often, it was a long time since he had gone far from Siena. Having then arrived in Genoa, he painted a scene there, beside that of Pordenone, in which he succeeded very well, and yet not in such a manner that it could be counted among his best works.[1] But, since the ways of the Court did not please him, being used to a life of freedom, he did not stay very willingly in that place, and, indeed, appeared as if he were stupefied. Wherefore, having come to the end of that work, he sought leave of the Prince and set out to return home; and passing by Pisa, in order to see that city, he met with Battista del Cervelliera and was shown all the most noteworthy things in the city, and in particular the altarpieces of Sogliani and the pictures that are in the recess behind the high altar of the Duomo.

Meanwhile Sebastiano della Seta, the Warden of Works of the Duomo, having heard from Cervelliera of the qualities and abilities of Domenico, and being desirous to finish the work so long delayed by Giovanni Antonio Sogliani, allotted two of the pictures for that recess to Domenico, to

[1] Lost

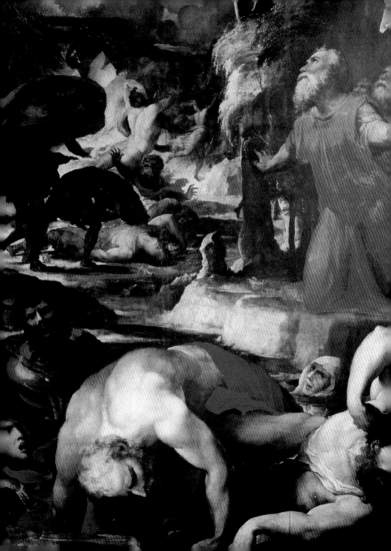

the end that he might execute them at Siena and send them finished to Pisa; and so it was done. In one is Moses, who, having found that the people had sacrificed to the Golden Calf, is breaking the Tables;[1] and in this Domenico painted some nudes that are figures of great beauty. In the other is the same Moses, with the earth opening and swallowing up a part of the people; and in this, also, are some nudes killed by flaming thunderbolts, which are marvellous.[2] These pictures, when taken to Pisa, led to Domenico painting four pictures for the front of that recess – namely, two on each side of the four Evangelists, which were four very beautiful figures.[3] Whereupon Sebastiano della Seta, who saw that he had been served quickly and well, commissioned Domenico, after these pictures, to paint the altarpiece of one of the chapels in the Duomo, Sogliani having by that time painted four. Settling in Pisa, therefore, Domenico painted in that altarpiece Our Lady in the sky with the Child in her arms, upon some clouds supported by some little Angels, with many Saints both male and female below, all executed passing well, but yet not with that perfection

[1], [2] & [3] Still in situ

Opposite: Moses and the Punishment of Korah, 1541

which marked the pictures described above.[1] But he, excusing himself for this to many of his friends, and particularly on one occasion to Giorgio Vasari, said that since he was away from the air of Siena and from certain comforts of his own, he did not seem to be able to do anything.

Having therefore returned home, determined that he would never again go away to work elsewhere, he painted for the nuns of S. Paolo, near S. Marco, an altarpiece in oils of the Nativity of Our Lady, with some nurses, and St Anne in a bed that is foreshortened and represented as standing within a door; and in a dark shadow is a woman who is drying clothes, without any other light but that which comes from the blaze of the fire.[2] In the predella, which is full of charm, are three scenes in tempera – the Presentation of the Virgin at the Temple, her Marriage, and the Adoration of the Magi. In the Mercanzia, a tribunal in that city, the officials have a little altarpiece which they say was painted by Domenico when he was young; it is very beautiful, and it contains in the centre a St Paul seated, and on

[1] Destroyed in 1596 [2] Pinacoteca Nazionale, Siena. Predella in private collection, England

Opposite: Nativity of the Virgin, c. 1530

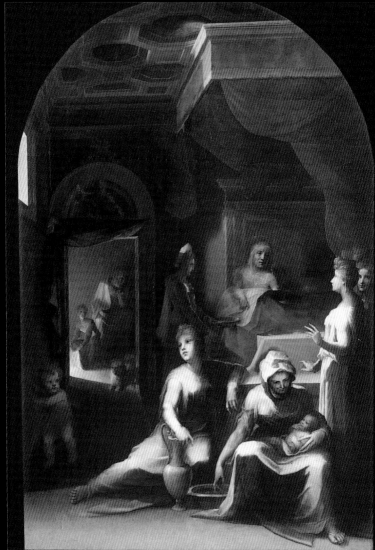

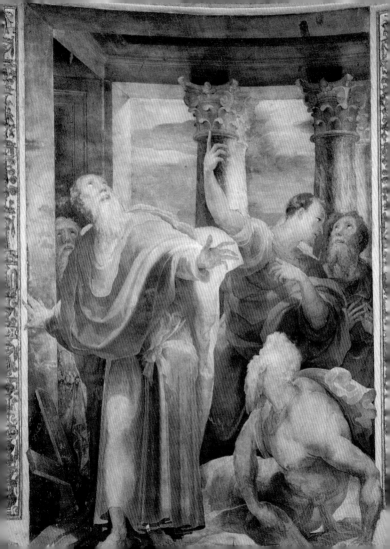

one side his Conversion, in little figures, and on the other the scene of his Beheading.[1]

Finally, Domenico was commissioned to paint the great recess of the Duomo, which is at the end behind the high altar.[2] In this he first made a decoration of stucco with foliage and figures, all with his own hand, and two Victories in the vacant spaces in the semicircle; which decoration was in truth a very rich and beautiful work. Then in the centre he painted in fresco the Ascension of Christ into Heaven; and from the cornice downwards he painted three pictures divided by columns in relief, and executed in perspective. In the middle picture, which has above it an arch in perspective, are Our Lady, St Peter, and St John; and in the spaces at the sides are ten Apostles, five on each side, all in various attitudes and gazing at Christ, who is ascending into Heaven; and above each of the two pictures of the Apostles is an Angel in foreshortening, the two together representing those two Angels who, after the Ascension, declared that He had risen into

[1] Museo dell'Opera del Duomo, Siena; see p. 10   [2] These paintings are still in situ, except for the central section, which was destroyed in an earthquake

Opposite: Apostles witnessing the Ascension, 1535-44

Heaven. This work is certainly admirable, but it would have been even more so if Domenico had given beautiful expressions to the heads; as it is, they have something in the expressions that is not very pleasing, and it appears that in his old age he adopted for his countenances an expression of terror by no means agreeable. This work, I say, if there had been any beauty in the heads, would have been so beautiful that there would have been nothing better to be seen. But in this matter of the expressions of the heads, in the opinion of the people of Siena, Sodoma was superior to Domenico, for the reason that Sodoma made them much more beautiful, although those of Domenico had more design and greater force. And, in truth, the manner of the heads in these our arts is of no little importance, and by painting them with graceful and beautiful expressions many masters have escaped the censure that they might have incurred for the rest of their work.

This was the last work in painting executed by Domenico, who, having taken it into his head in the end to work in relief, began to give his attention to casting in bronze, and went so far with this that he executed, although with extraordinary labour, six

Opposite: Angel Candelabrum, 1548

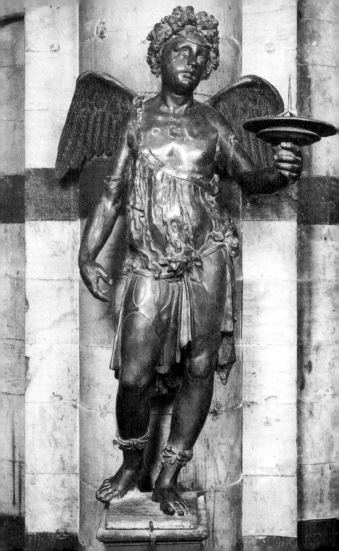

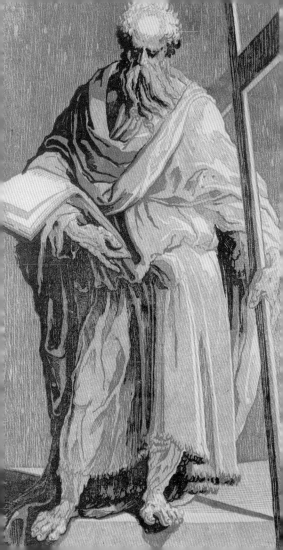

Angels of bronze in the round, little less than life size, for the six columns nearest the high altar of the Duomo. These Angels, which are very beautiful, are holding *tazze*, or rather little basins, which support candelabra containing lights, and in the last of them he acquitted himself so well, that he was very highly praised for them. Whereupon, growing in courage, he made a beginning with figures of the twelve Apostles, which were to be placed on the columns lower down, where there are now some of marble, old and in a bad manner; but he did not continue them, for he did not live long after that. And since he was a man of infinite ingenuity, and succeeded well in everything, he engraved wood-blocks by himself in order to make prints in chiaroscuro, and there are to be seen prints of two Apostles engraved by him excellently well, of which we have one in our book of drawings, together with some sheets drawn divinely by his hand.[2] He also engraved copperplates with the burin, and he etched some very fanciful little stories of alchemy, in which Jove and the other Gods, wishing to congeal

[1] Eight angels still in situ, Duomo, Siena. [2] A sheet of draw-ings as assembled by Vasari survives in the Louvre, Paris

Opposite: St. Philip, chiaroscuro print, c. 1540

Mercury, place him bound in a crucible, and Vulcan and Pluto make fire around him; but when they think that he must be fixed, Mercury flies away and goes off in smoke.

Domenico, in addition to the works described above, executed many others of no great importance, pictures of the Madonna and other such-like chamber-pictures, such as a Madonna that is in the house of the Chevalier Donati, and a picture in tempera in which Jove changes himself into a shower of gold and rains into the lap of Danaë. Piero Catanei, likewise, has a round picture in oils of a very beautiful Virgin by the hand of the same master. He also painted a most beautiful bier for the Confraternity of S. Lucia, and likewise another for that of S. Antonio; nor should anyone be astonished that I make mention of such works, for or the reason that they are beautiful to a marvel, as all know who have seen them.

Finally, having come to the age of sixty-five, he hastened the end of his life by toiling all by himself day and night at his castings in metal, polishing them himself without calling in any assistance. He died, then, on the 18th of May, 1549, and was given burial by his dearest friend, the goldsmith Giuliano, in the Duomo, where he had executed so many rare works. And he was carried to the tomb by all the craftsmen of his city, which recognized even then the great loss that she had suffered in the death of Domenico. And now, as she admires his works, recognizes it more than ever.

Domenico was an orderly and upright person, fearing God and studious in his art, although solitary beyond measure; wherefore he well deserved to be honourably celebrated by his fellow-citizens of Siena, who have always won great praise by their attention to noble studies and to poetry, with verses both in Latin and in the vulgar tongue.

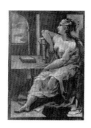

Illustrations

Cover: Self-Portrait of Beccafumi, c. 1527, oil on paper,
31.3 x 22.6 cm, Uffizi, Florence

p. 1: Lucretia (fragment), c. 1518, oil on wood,
Oberlin College, Oberlin

p. 2 Virgin and Child with St. John the Baptist, c. 1541, oil on wood,
90 x 65 cm, Galleria Nazionale d'Arte Antica, Rome

p. 4 Zeuxis and the Young Women of Croton, 1519, fresco,
250 x 280 cm, Palazzo Bindi Sergardi, Siena

p. 6: St. Bernardino preaching, 1535-37, tempera on wood,
30 x 50.5 cm, Musée du Louvre, Paris

p. 7: St. Catherine receiving the habit of the Order of St. Dominic,
1514-15, tempera on wood, 31 x 49 cm, Pinacoteca Nazionale, Siena

p. 10: St Paul Enthroned, 1516-17, tempera and oil on wood,
230 x 150 cm, Museo dell'Opera del Duomo, Siena

p. 12: The Cult of Ceres (Ceralia), 1519, oil on wood,
67 x 125 cm, Martelli Collection, Florence

p. 13: The Festival of Lupercalia, 1519, oil on wood,
67 x 125 cm, Martelli Collection, Florence

p. 14: Elijah and Ahab, marble inlay floor, c. 1524,
350 x 350 cm, Duomo, Siena

p. 17: Study of old man, oil on paper, c. 1524, 26.9 x 19.9 cm,
Fogg Art Museum, Cambridge, Mass.

p. 18: Virgin and Child with St. Jerome and the Infant St. John,
c. 1519, oil on wood, diameter 85.5 cm,
Thyssen-Bornemisza Collection, Madrid

p. 21: St. Catherine receiving the Stigmata, c. 1545, oil on wood,
55 x 40 cm, Boymans-van Beuningen Museum, Rotterdam

p. 25: Portrait of Beccafumi from original edition of Vasari's *Lives*

p. 26: Tanaquil, c. 1519, oil on wood, 92 x 53 cm,
National Gallery, London

p. 30: Sketch for a façade decoration for the Borghesi, c. 1512,
ink and wash over pencil, 41.7 x 20 cm,
British Museum, London

p. 33: St Catharine receiving the Stigmata, 1514-1515,
tempera and oil on wood, 212 x 162 cm,
Pinacoteca Nazionale, Siena

First published 2007 by
Pallas Athene,
42 Spencer Rise,
London NW5 1AP

www.pallasathene.co.uk

ISBN 1 84368 028 9/978 1 84368 028 4

Printed in China

This book is part of our series
Lives of the Artists,
presenting biographies of artists by their contemporaries,
many of them published for the first time.
To find out more visit our website,
www.livesoftheartists.co.uk

Note on the text:

The text used here is the translation by Gaston de Vere,
who took great pains to stay close to Vasari's idiom.
First published in 1912, its Edwardian Renaissance prose
has a flavour of its own, and we have made only
the smallest number of modernisations.

THE

I F
LOCO

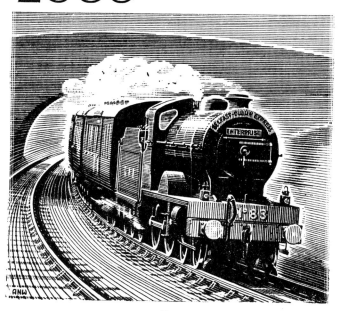

By

R. N. CLEMENTS and J. M. ROBBINS

LONDON :

Ian Allan Ltd

1949

Preface

IRISH railways are a source of great interest to the railway enthusiast. Much of the rolling stock dates back into the last century. The modern trend towards standardisation has dealt less ruthlessly with locomotives and carriages than is the case in Great Britain. Many of the engines and vehicles, some of which are fully sixty years old, have undergone interesting changes during the process of rebuilding. One reason for the retention of so much of the stock belonging to a past age has been the difficulties of the last eight or nine years, when materials have been almost impossible to obtain. Moreover, it has been necessary for certain companies operating in the Six Counties to work their stock to the utmost capacity to cope with the heavy traffic in passengers and freight during the war years. Even this summer (1948) the railways have been hard put to it to find sufficient engines and coaches to meet public demands.

During the war period very little new stock was obtained. The N.C.C. had four engines built, 2-6-0s Nos. 101 to 104—while two shunting tanks (Nos. 18 and 19) were obtained second-hand from the L.M.S. During the past eighteen months the N.C.C. had ten 2-6-4 tank engines built at Derby. On the G.N.R. (I) no engines were built during the war years, but during 1948 fifteen new engines were delivered by Messrs. Beyer, Peacock—five 3-cylinder 4-4-0 express engines, five 4-4-0 engines for branch lines and five 0-6-0 mixed traffic engines. On the B. & C.D. Rly. one new tank engine, No. 9, was delivered from Messrs. Beyer, Peacock in 1945. No new locomotives were built by the C.I.E. after 1939 until the latter end of 1947, when the first of five new Diesel shunting locomotives was turned out from their Inchicore Works.

It should be mentioned that the standard Irish gauge is 5 ft. 3 in., but there are a number of light railways of 3 ft. 0 in. gauge, some of which form part of the C.I.E. The best known of the independent concerns are the County Donegal Railways (jointly owned by the G.N. and N.C.C.) and the Londonderry and Lough Swilly Company. Mention should be made of the successful efforts of the late Mr. Henry Forbes, General Manager of the County Donegal Railways, to attract traffic by a comparatively frequent service maintained by small petrol railcars. These were replaced by diesel cars in attractive livery of bright red lower panels with cream uppers.

Many changes have taken place since the first issue of the A.B.C. of Irish Locomotives. The last portion (Letterkenny to Gweedore) of line between Letterkenny and Burtonport was closed on 6th January, 1946, while during the first week in January, 1948, the Bessbrook and Newry electric tramway closed down owing to competition by road. On the County Donegal Railway, the section from Stranorlar to Glenties was closed on 13th December, 1947, for passenger and freight traffic, but is being kept open for special trains of turf and cattle. On the C.I.E. a number of branch lines were closed to traffic during the war period, and some have not yet been re-opened. It is a matter for conjecture whether they will be brought into use again or be permanently closed.

The train services, particularly in Eire, are not so frequent as in 1939. A bad set-back occurred during the winters of 1946-47, due to the coal troubles in England. Neither on the C.I.E., G.N., nor N.C.C. are the booked times of express trains as fast as in 1939, but generally speaking the loads are heavier, and there are many slacks for renovations to track, so for these reasons the timings are on the generous side.

Very few industrial concerns own locomotives in Ireland, but those which do have had their locomotive stock included in this book. Some of the engines are of great interest, such as those belonging to Messrs. Arthur Guinness, Son & Co., and the Irish Sugar Company.

Coras Iompair Eireann

Coras Iompair Eireann, or the Transport Company of Ireland, came into being in 1945, when the former Great Southern Railways Company amalgamated with the Dublin United Transport Company and the present name was adopted by the newly formed concern. All road and rail transport came under the monopoly of C.I.E., except in the areas under the jurisdiction of the G.N.R. (I). A change of administration likewise took place. Though the concern is a private one, with a board of directors, yet the Government guarantees debenture interest and has assumed to itself the right to appoint the chairman.

In 1925 all railway companies working exclusively in Eire had been amalgamated into the Great Southern Railways. The lines absorbed in this undertaking were the G.S. & W., the M.G.W., the D.S.E. and C.B. & S.C. Railways, to name the chief ones. A number of smaller companies were included, mostly light railways of 3 ft. 0 in., such as the Cavan & Leitrim and the West Clare. Amalgamation was nothing new to the G.S. & W. Railway as in 1900 it absorbed the Waterford and Central Ireland and a year later the Waterford, Limerick & Western Railway.

C.I.E.

Of all the companies constituting the G.S. Railways, the earliest was the D.S.E.R., which included the original Dublin and Kingstown Railway opened in 1834. The next on the list was the G.S. & W., which was opened as far as Carlow in 1846. The M.G.W.R. started its career one year later, 1847, when the first section to Enfield was opened for traffic.

The accompanying map will show the area covered by the C.I.E., which operates 2,612½ miles of track (including sidings) and is responsible for transport, both rail and road, in the greater part of Eire, including the City of Dublin. The G.N.R. (I) covers the territory to the North of Dublin and West of Dundalk.

The financial condition of C.I.E. has not been satisfactory, the G.S. Railways having been badly affected by road competition, and by the difficulties caused by the late war. Little development has taken place in the matter of construction, no new locomotives having been built since the three 4-6-0s of the 800 class (1939-40) until the advent of the new Diesel shunting engine No. 1000 in November 1947. No new coaches have been constructed. The fuel difficulties of 1946-48 caused the conversion of 97 engines to burn oil fuel, at great expense ; but these engines have been reconverted to use coal. Hopes are being expressed that the railway departments of the concern may be brought up to date by the introduction of new Diesel main line engines, new coaching stock, new marshalling yards and reconstruction of stations and goods stores.

The peak of railway services was reached during the summer of 1939. With the advent of the 800 class of express passenger locomotive a number of accelerations were made, particularly in the case of the up and down mails between Dublin and Cork. Some very sharp bookings were laid down, such as the 20½ miles from Thurles to Limerick Junction, scheduled in 22 minutes, which included a stop outside the station to set back to the platform. Again, the 37½ miles from Limerick Junction to Mallow were booked to be covered in 40 minutes. The longest non-stop runs were (and are) between Dublin and Thurles, 86½ miles, the best pre-war booking being 97 minutes in the up direction. The 800 class was fully equal to the task imposed upon it. Probably the best performance was on a test run when No. 800 hauled a train of 15 bogies unassisted from Cork to Mallow. This was a notable achievement in view of the start from Cork, which commences at the end of Glanmire Road station platform with a gradient of 1 in 78, steepening to 1 in 60 for two miles after passing through the tunnel. The train service at the present time has improved to a considerable extent, but the present running speeds are by no means equal to those operating in 1939. The principal trains on the Dublin and Cork main line are always worked by locomotives of the 800, 400 and 500 classes of 4-6-0 and the 321 class of 4-4-0.

On the other main lines the trains have never been so speedily timed, owing more to the curvature of the track than to steep

4

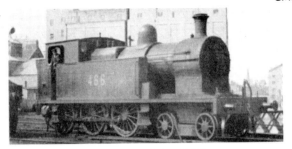

No. 466, Class B4 : 4-6-0T ex-C.B. & S.C.R.   [*J. M. Robbins*

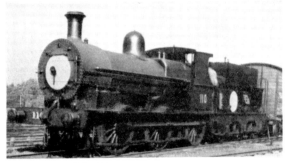

No. 110, Class J15 oil burner   [*R. N. Clements*

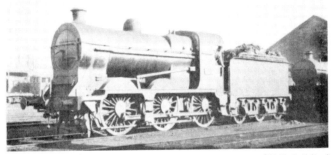

No. 625, Class J5   [*W. H. C. Kelland*

5

1

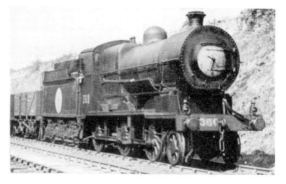

2

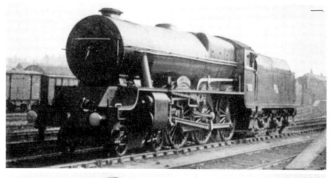

3

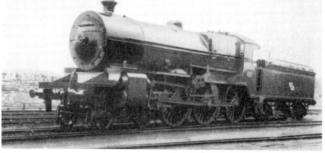

C.I.E.

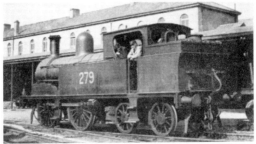

Top : 0-4-4T
No. 279, Class
E1
   H. C. Casserley

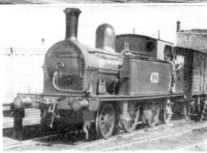

Right: 2-4-2T
(ex-D.S.E.R.)
No. 433, Class
F2, in green
livery
   [*J. M. Robbins*

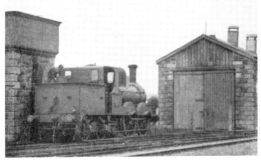

0-4-4T No. 47
Class E3.
Class now
extinct.
   [*H. C. Casserley*

Key to photos opposite :

(1) Class K3 2-6-0 No. 360 near Inchicore   [*R. Casserley*
(2) Class B1a 4-6-0 No. 801, *Macha*   [*H. C. Casserley*
(3) Class B2 4-6-0 No. 405 in new green livery with C.I.E. emblem on
        tender   [*R. N. Clements*

7

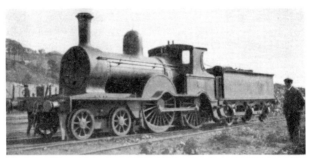

C.I.E. (*Top*) No. 98, Class D17
(*Centre*) No. 545, Class D5 (ex-M.G.W.R.)
(*Bottom*) No. 330, Class D2

[*W. H. C. Kelland*
[*R. N. Clements*
[*J. M. Robbins*

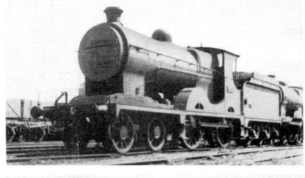

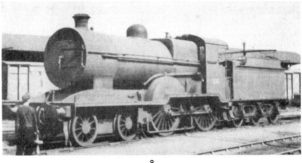

gradients. To effect economies the section between Clonsilla and Ballinasloe is now single, though formerly it was double. At all crossing-places one track has been straightened out to permit fast running in both directions. Engines allocated to the M.G.W. section are the " Woolwich " 2-6-0s of the 372 and 393 classes and 4-4-0s of the 540 and 550 classes. On the Dublin-Wexford and Rosslare Harbour-Mallow lines no fast timings are permissible owing to severe gradients and the number of stops.

On the whole the gradients on the main line between Dublin and Cork are relatively easy except for the start from Kingsbridge station at 1 in 84 to Inchicore and a steady though somewhat less steep rise to Clondalkin, and again the stiff gradients at the Cork end.

For the student of railways, there is much of interest to be seen on the C.I.E. Even if large locomotives are the exception rather than the rule, yet many existing types are fully sixty years old and are doing first-class work, several of these being in the Dublin area. Similarly, due to difficulties in obtaining supplies of raw materials, it has been necessary to retain many ancient coaches in service ; there are many interesting types to be seen, belonging to the companies which formed the G.S.R., and even several which were built for the Waterford, Limerick and Western Railway.

C.I.E. LOCOMOTIVES

The locomotive stock of C.I.E. comprises a wide variety ; when the G.S.R. was formed in 1925 the 587 locomotives were divided into no less than 114 different classes, though on account of the considerable degree of standardisation and interchangeability of parts on both the G.S. & W.R. and the M.G.W.R. the situation was not quite as bad as appears at first ; these two companies between them accounted for 61 classes, but the remaining 53 classes were a very mixed lot, averaging barely over two engines per class (114 engines).

Since 1925 42 classes have disappeared, but the addition of some new ones still leaves the total at 83 classes for 491 engines.

For many years all engines, with the exception of the 800 class of 1939-40, were painted dark grey, but the larger passenger engines, and also the Dublin suburban tank engines and Diesel locomotives, are now being painted green.

In the tables on pages 21-4, in addition to the class, the type of boiler carried by each engine is shown, though it should be understood that these are liable to variation as engines go through the shops. The classification of boilers has been slightly simplified compared with the official version.

Boilers classified by letter are superheated, except E, S, T and U, and are Belpaire, except E and S.

Those classified by engine class numbers are saturated, except 257, 400, 461, 530 and 650 classes (the two latter exist in both

ABBREVIATIONS USED THROUGHOUT

B.C.D.R.	...	...	Belfast and County Down Railway
C.B.S.C.R.	...	...	Cork, Bandon and South Coast Railway
C.D.R.	...	...	County Donegal Railways
C.D.R.J.C.	...	...	County Donegal Railways Joint Committee
C.I.E.	...	...	Coras Iompair Eireann (Transport Company of Eire)
C. & L.	...	...	Cavan & Leitrim Railway
C.V.R.	...	...	Clogher Valley Railway
D.N. & G.R.	...	...	Dundalk, Newry and Greenore Railway
D.S.E.R.	...	...	Dublin and South Eastern Railway
G.N.R.	...	...	Great Northern Railway
G.S.R.	...	...	Great Southern Railways
G.S. & W.R.	...	...	Great Southern and Western Railway
L. & L.S.R.	...	...	Londonderry and Lough Swilly Railway
M.G.W.R.	...	...	Midland and Great Western Railway
N.C.C.	...	...	Northern Counties Committee (late L.M.S.R.)
N.G.	...	...	Narrow Gauge
S.L. & N.C.R.	...	...	Sligo, Leitrim and Northern Counties Railway
W.C.	...	...	West Clare Railway
W.L.W.R.	...	...	Waterford, Limerick and Western Railway
W. & T.	...	...	Waterford & Tramore Railway

saturated and superheated form) and are round-top boilers, except classes 400, 448, 451, 461, 594 and 700.

G.S. & W.R.

Taking first the ex-G.S. & W.R. stock, which was not renumbered in 1925, the influence of Alexander MacDonnell, who was Locomotive Superintendent from 1864 to 1883, is still to the fore ; MacDonnell carried standardisation to a very great length, and even after his departure all engines built to the end of the nineteenth century were practically to his standard designs, though enlarged.

None of his 2-4-0 passenger now remain, but the 2 class branch line engines (D19) differed from his 2-4-0 engines only in having a bogie (they were the first 4-4-0 engines in Ireland) ; several are still in service, though all now carry modern Belpaire boilers. Similarly the 52 class (D17), actually built by Aspinall immediately after MacDonnell's departure, are a bogie version of MacDonnell's last 2-4-0 express engines, and Ivatt's 60 class (D14) are an enlarged version of the same design. From 1900 on, Coey built much larger 4-4-0 engines, culminating in the 321 class (D2) of 1904 ; from 1903 on, all Coey's passenger engines had taper boilers, but these have now all been replaced by parallel Belpaire boilers. The 321 class rebuilt with new frames and boilers still do a share of the main line express work ; an unusual feature of these and most of the other older engines rebuilt with superheaters is the continued use of slide valves, which have proved quite satisfactory ; No. 332 of this class, however, differs in having been rebuilt with piston valves.

A similar series, the 333 class (D3), was built in 1907-8 for the Rosslare road, having 5 ft. 8½ in. driving wheels and a smaller firebox; five more (342 class) were built by the G.S.R. in 1936, similar to the rebuilt 333 class except for an increase in wheelbase and the provision of piston valves ; No. 338 of the rebuilds (D2) is also a piston valve engine.

In 1914 E. A. Watson, who had come to Inchicore from the G.W.R., decided to introduce 4-cylinder 4-6-0 engines. The first of them, No. 400, appeared in 1916 and nine more were added in 1921-2. In their original form they were not too satisfactory and some have been rebuilt with two cylinders. First came an extensive rebuild of No. 402, which was almost a new engine, and Nos. 401 and 406 were similarly rebuilt, but with Caprotti gear instead of piston valves. These three were re-classified as B2a. The result was very satisfactory, but for reasons of economy a less extensive rebuild was made of the other four engines (three had been scrapped) ; standard 19½ in. by 28 in. cylinders were again used, but with recessed covers permitting retention of the 26 in. stroke of the original engines, and the frames were new only in front of the leading coupled axle. The final improvement was the fitting of four engines with the much larger K boiler introduced in 1937.

For goods traffic the G.S. & W.R. had one of the most remarkably successful classes of engine ever built ; the 101 class 0-6-0 (J15) were introduced in 1866 and from then till 1903 no less than 111 were built, though of course the later engines had larger boilers and cylinders. To-day, over 80 years after their introduction, they are still by far the most numerous class of engine in Ireland, 96 being still in service, of which 61 have modern Z class superheater boilers.

The same year as the last of the 101 class were built (1903), Coey produced two much larger types of 0-6-0, the 351 class (J9) and the still larger 355 class (K3) ; the latter were soon rebuilt as 2-6-0 engines, and as further rebuilt and superheated are still on heavy main line goods work. In 1907 Coey produced the first Irish 4-6-0, an inside cylinder goods engine, but he finally returned to the 2-6-0 type (K4) and all the 4-6-0 goods engines have been withdrawn.

The 257 class (J4) of 1913 was a superheated version of the 351 class for lighter goods work and finally in 1924 Mr. Bazin introduced the 500 class of 4-6-0 with outside cylinders and 5 ft. 8½ in. driving wheels, but though originally intended as mixed traffic engines they proved so successful on express work that they have been so employed ever since.

Of passenger tank engines the oldest remaining are the 2-4-2T of the 33 class (F6). Though not built till 1892 they are a tank version of MacDonnell's 2-4-0 engines of 1873 ; from 1894 on they were built with bogies as the 37 class (C7), exactly corresponding to the 2 class tender engines. The larger 4-4-2T of the 27 class (C4) are a tank version of the 52 class engines, but with driving wheels 5 ft. 8½ in. instead of 6 ft. 7 in. These were the last passenger tank engines built by the G.S. & W.R.

Mention should also be made of the diminutive 0-6-0T engines

C.I.E.

Nos. 90 and 100. In 1875 MacDonnell built a 0-6-4T rail motor for use on the Castleisland railway ; this was a combined engine and carriage with accommodation for both first and third class passengers in the carriage portion over the bogie. Two more were subsequently built, of which one continued to work between Inchicore and Kingsbridge till 1945. In 1890 two similar small 0-6-0T were built for use on the light permanent way of the Fermoy and Mitchelstown branch; these were without the carriage portion, and this was subsequently removed from No. 90, which thus also became a 0-6-0T.

Of the goods tank engines few require special mention. No. 204 and " Jumbo " are rebuilds of MacDonnell's 0-6-4T banking engines. The 213 class (I1) are a tank version of the 351 class 0-6-0, with smaller driving wheels ; there were originally four of these engines, but two were rebuilt as 0-6-0 tender engines (J3).

Finally there are still a few survivors of the 58 engines taken over in 1901 with the Waterford, Limerick & Western Railway ; these are classes C5, D15, E1, E2, G3 and J25, twelve engines in all.

M.G.W.R.

Although the characteristic outline of the older M.G.W. engines with Atock's turned-up cab and bell-mouthed cast-iron chimneys has completely disappeared, all the classes taken over from the M.G.W.R. in 1925 still exist, with one exception.

The oldest passenger engines are the 530 class (D16), rebuilt in 1900-1 from small 2-4-0s of 1880 ; next are the 650 class (G2), Atock's standard passenger engine of 1893. These are notable in several respects : they are probably the last class of 2-4-0 in existence of which no engine has yet been scrapped (with the exception of one which was a victim of the Civil War of 1922) and they are possibly the only superheated 2-4-0s. They are very free-running little engines and in spite of their driving wheels being only 5 ft. 8 in. diameter, have been timed at speeds close to 70 m.p.h.

In 1902 Cusack introduced the " Celtic " class of 4-4-0 express engines, then the largest engines in Ireland, which as rebuilt with superheaters and piston valves are now class D5. A smaller type of 4-4-0 engine was introduced in 1909, now all rebuilt with boilers similar to the D5 class, but shorter and with much smaller fireboxes. These are now classes D6 (piston valve) and D7 (slide valve) and were the last M.G.W.R. passenger engines.

Of the goods engines No. 567 is interesting. The 5 ft. 2 in. driving wheels of this class (of which there were originally six engines) were not a standard size of the M.G.W.R.; the reason is that as built in 1879 the engines incorporated parts (including the driving wheels) of some Fairbairn 0-4-2 engines of 1860 ; a second heavy rebuild of 1899 removed any remaining parts of the 1860 engines, but the survival of this non-standard size of driving wheels is directly attributable to the old Fairbairns. All the other engines of the class were condemned in 1925, but No. 567 survived on account of having been rebuilt with new boiler and piston valves in 1919 for experiments with the Cusack-Morton firebox superheater. Actually the oldest M.G.W. goods engines are the Avonside class of 1880, now J6. These were obtained very cheap from the Avonside Engine Co., who had built them in 1878 for the Waterford, Dungarvan & Lismore Railway, but were left with them on their hands when that Company refused delivery owing to the engines not being ready in time. They were a remarkable bargain, as after a heavy rebuild in 1906-8, and subsequent addition of superheaters and piston-valves, three are still on main line goods trains, and the fourth was only withdrawn in 1945 after 65 years work.

The standard M.G.W. goods engines, numbering 42 at the amalgamation, were all similar except that the earlier ones had been rebuilt with Belpaire boilers ; these became J19 (594 class) and the later ones, which retained their round-top boilers, became J18 (573 class). As most have now been rebuilt with standard superheater X boilers, and the 573 and 594 class boilers are used indiscriminately in the two classes, there has ceased to be any real difference between them, though there are considerable external differences. No. 575 is the last survivor of the earliest batch of these engines, dating from 1876; all the others were built between 1885 and 1895.

In 1901 the M.G.W.R. took two 0-6-0 engines ordered from Kitson by the W.L.W.R. which were not required by the G.S. & W.R.: in the 1925 renumbering these were allotted numbers in the G.S. & W. list, along with the similar W.L.W.R. engines; hence the remaining one is No. 234. The larger M.G.W.R. goods engines built in 1904, and corresponding to the " Celtic " class of 4-4-0 are all scrapped, which leaves only the " F " class 0-6-0 of 1924 (now J5). These were mixed traffic engines: their 5 ft. 8 in. wheel was large enough to work the fastest trains on the M.G.W.R. when required, and they were equally suitable for cattle and goods traffic, and can still be found in charge of most of the M.G.W. section goods trains as well as doing a fair share of passenger work.

Of tank engines the M.G.W.R. had only two types, both 0-6-0. J10 were a tank version of the standard goods engines, with smaller wheels, which were built in 1881-5 for shunting at the North Wall and banking Down goods trains thence, and have remained on those duties ever since. J26 are small engines originally intended for working mixed trains on branch lines ; they are now to be found as shunting engines all over the C.I.E. and Nos. 553, 555 and 560 work the Waterford & Tramore section.

D.S.E.R.

Of the D.S.E.R. passenger tender engines, only one remains, No. 454 Class D8. Of goods tender engines there are four 0-6-0s,

C.I.E.

consisting originally of three slightly different lots, but now all classed J8 (for nearly 30 years these were the only engines in Ireland with side-window cabs), and one engine, No. 448, class J1, which was originally a 0-6-2T, but was rebuilt as a tender engine in 1908 owing to the weight being found excessive. Finally there are Mr. Wild's two fine 2-6-0 engines of 1922 (the only superheated engines on the D.S.E.R.), both of which have remained ever since on their original duties on the Wexford goods.

The three 2-4-0T engines are survivors of what was for many years the standard suburban tank engine ; there were 12 engines in the class, the largest number the D.S.E.R. ever possessed of one class. Nos. 430-433 of class F2 are rebuilds of this type and are identical with it except for the trailing wheels and larger bunkers and tanks, but No. 428 differed in being built as a 2-4-2T. Class F1 were the later design of 2-4-2T, of which some originally had Belpaire boilers.

The older 4-4-2T, class C3, were built by Sharp Stewart in 1893 to deal with the increased traffic due to the opening of the loop line. Class C2 are much more modern engines ; No. 455 was the first of them and was Mr. Cronin's last engine. It is interesting as being the last engine built at Grand Canal Street Works. In 1841 the Dublin & Kingstown Railway built the 2-2-2T " Princess " there, and this was the first engine in the world built by a railway company in their own works. The other two engines of class C2, Nos. 456-7, were added by Mr. Wild in 1924 and originally had Belpaire fireboxes.

C.B.S.C.R.

The only surviving type of C.B.S.C.R. engines are the fine 4-6-0T built by Beyer-Peacock, all but one of those running having been rebuilt with new superheater boilers. Most are used for goods traffic on the Bandon section, but one is usually to be found on the D.S.E. suburban services.

There are also the two small engines " Argadeen " and " St. Molaga," which belonged to the Timoleague & Courtmacsherry Railway and which have remained there, retaining their names and without numbers. The reason for their survival is that only very light engines can work this standard gauge light railway, though the small G.S. & W. engines Nos. 90, 100 and 299 are also used on it. " Argadeen " is interesting in that its present boiler is one formerly carried by a 0-4-0T (now scrapped) which was a D.S.E.R. rail motor engine. The boiler was, however, lengthened when transferred to " Argadeen," so that it is not quite equal to the feat of the C.B.S.C.R., who at one moment had both 2-4-0T and 4-6-0T engines carrying boilers of identical dimensions.

G.S.R.

The number of new engines built by the G.S.R. since 1925 was small, owing to the financial position of the Company and decreasing traffic due to road competition. First came the Woolwich 2-6-0 engines of the 372 and 393 classes (K1 and K1a) ; twelve sets of parts had been bought by the M.G.W.R. before the amalgamation, and the G.S.R. bought 15 more, though actually only 26 engines appeared from 1925 to 1930, of which the last six had 6 ft. driving wheels.

During 1927 two small Sentinel engines were obtained for shunting and the same year saw the purchase of a number of steam rail-cars ; all these have been withdrawn, as have four Drewry petrol cars. Another shunting engine, No. 495, 0-4-0T, by Peckett, was bought from Allman & Co., of Bandon, in 1930 for use on the quays at Cork.

In 1928 came the large outside cylinder 2-6-2T for the D.S.E. section, No. 850, a design which was not perpetuated.

From 1929 to 1935 appeared 15 0-6-0 goods engines which, as their classification shows, are modernised versions of the 101 class. The 700 class (J15a) of 1929 were saturated engines with larger boilers than the 101 class, but the 710 class (J15b) of 1934-5, superheated and with piston valves, had the same Z boiler as was used for the rebuilding of the 101 class. In 1933 five 0-6-2T engines had been built for the D.S.E. section suburban traffic (670 class) ; these are very similar to the 710 class 0-6-0, but with driving wheels 5 ft. 6in. diameter.

In 1936 came the 342 class general purpose passenger engines already referred to and finally in 1939 the three magnificent 3-cylinder 4-6-0 engines of the 800 class ; with the sole exception of the G.W.R. Kings these are probably the largest and most powerful 4-6-0 engines on this side of the Atlantic ; their introduction permitted a considerable acceleration of the Cork Mail trains, and even the new schedules were far within their powers. Unfortunately the war came before they were long in service and since then the coal shortage has prevented the introduction of any schedules proportionate to their ability.

War conditions have also prevented any new construction since 1940, with the exception of the five Diesel shunting engines Nos. 1000-1004 assembled by C.I.E. at Inchicore during 1947-8 ; further Diesels are at present under construction and on order, including six main line engines of 1,830 b.h.p.

NARROW GAUGE

The West Clare Railway used unusual types of engine in the shape of 0-6-2T and 2-6-2T designs with inside frames throughout. A very peculiar feature of the 0-6-2T design is that the trailing wheels are the same size as the coupled wheels ; originally all were 4 ft., but this was reduced to the present size of 3 ft. 6 in.

All the later engines of this line were variations of the 4-6-0T type with outside frames throughout and outside cylinders which proved very satisfactory on the L.L.S.R. and C.D.R.J.C., and appears to have been the type of engine encouraged by the Board of Works. The last two, class BN3, have Walschaerts valve gear.

The Cavan & Leitrim Railway used 4-4-0T engines, a popular type on several of the narrow gauge lines. Eight of these were obtained in 1887, and the company only found it necessary to get one more engine. This was a 0-6-4T obtained in 1904 (the only Irish narrow-gauge engine of this type), but it did relatively little work and was scrapped in 1934. All the C. & L. engines had relatively large fire-boxes, as the fuel used up to 1925 was the local Arigna coal.

In 1934 the C. & L. stock was augmented by the addition of four 2-4-2T engines transferred from the Cork, Blackrock & Passage section, which had been closed in 1932, and during the war Nos. 3T and 4T, both 2-6-0T engines, from the Tralee & Dingle, were brought to help deal with the increased coal traffic. Thus the present stock on this section consists of five of the original engines, three from the C.B.P. section (No. 11L was scrapped) and two from the Tralee & Dingle, 10 engines in all, which is one more than the C. & L. ever possessed in its independent days. Although the C.B.P. engines were renumbered when transferred, the T.D. engines retain their original numbers.

The Schull & Skibbereen never rose above four engines, of which two survive, both 4-4-0T. No. 4S, built by Nasmyth Wilson in 1888, is remarkable as having been the first engine in the British Isles with a Belpaire firebox, and the Walschaerts valve gear was also an exceptional feature at that date, though it was also used the next year by the Tralee & Dingle Railway.

No. 6S was transferred to the S.S. section to replace a 4-4-0T, which was scrapped. It is the last survivor of the Cork & Muskerry Light Railway stock, and the type 0-4-4T is also unique on an Irish narrow-gauge line. It was sent to Skibbereen in 1938 after having been out of service since the C.M.L.R. was closed in 1934.

The Tralee & Dingle used 2-6-0T and 2-6-2T engines, nearly all with Walschaerts valve gear. The original 2-6-0T engines obtained for the opening of the line were the most satisfactory, and after various experiments with other designs, the Company returned to this type for the last engine they obtained in 1910.

In the Tables throughout this booklet, boiler pressure is expressed in lb. per square inch, and tractive effort in lb. at 85 per cent. boiler pressure.

C.I.E.
NARROW GAUGE
LOCOMOTIVES

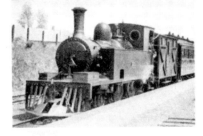

[J. Macartney Robbins

Above : Cavan & Leitrim section 4-4-0T No. 1L *Isabel* (Class DN2)

Left : Tralee & Dingle 2 - 6 - 2T No. 5T (Class PN2)

[R. N. Clements

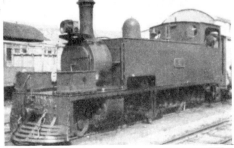

Right : Schull & Skibbereen 4-4-0T No. 4S (Class DN5)

Below : West Clare 0-6-2T No. 5C (Class IN1) at Ennis. Note the size of the trailing wheels—an Irish curiosity !

[Photos : H. C. Casserley

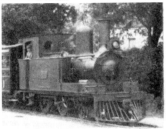

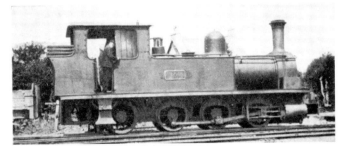

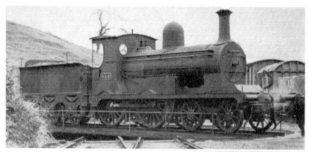

C.I.E. No. 530, Class D16

[H. C. Casserley

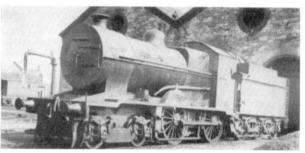

C.I.E. No. 344, Class D4

[R. N. Clements

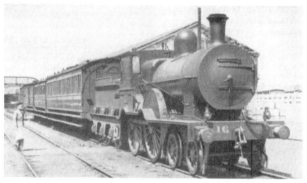

C.I.E. No. 16, Class D17, on Limerick train at Ennis   [J. M. Robbins

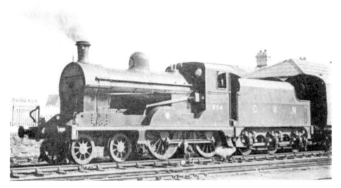

New light 4-4-0 No. 204 *Antrim*, Class U   [*H. C. Casserley*

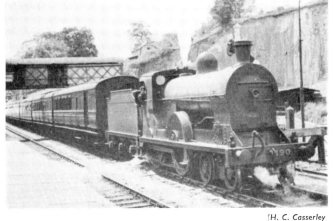

[*H. C. Casserley*

Class S2 4-4-0 No. 190, on a Dublin-Belfast train waiting at Goraghwood
for Customs examination

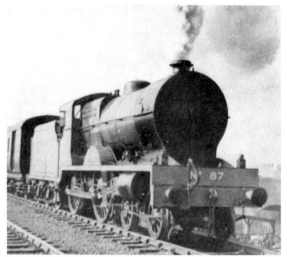

4-4-0 Class V Compound No. 87 *Kestrel*   [*J. M. Robbins*

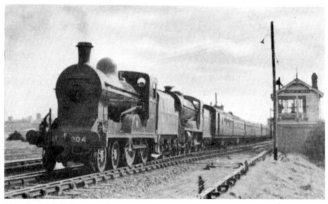

New light 4-4-0 No. 204 *Antrim* piloting 4-4-0 Compound No. 83 *Eagle*
on a Dublin-Belfast express, leaving Dundalk
[*H. C. Casserley*

C.I.E.

NUMERICAL LIST OF ENGINES, WITH CLASSES AND BOILER TYPES

No.	Class	Boiler	No.	Class	Boiler	No.	Class	Boiler	No.	Class	Boiler
1	D17	52*	65	D14	700*	134	J15	Z			
2	D19	U	85	D14	60*	135	J15	101*			
3	D17	52*	86	D14	Z	136	J15	Z			
4	D17	X	87	D14	60*	137	J15	Z			
5	D19	U	88	D14	Z	138	J15	Z			
6	D19	U	89	D14	Z	139	J15	Z			
7	D19	U	90	J30†	90	140	J15	Z			
9	D17	52*	93	D14	Z	141	J15	Z			
10	D19	U	94	D14	Z	143	J15	Z			
11	D17	52*	95	D14	Z	144	J15	Z			
12	D17	X	96	D14	Z	146	J15	Z			
13	D19	U	98	D17	52*	147	J15	Z			
14	D17	X	100	J30	90	148	J15	Z			
15	D19	U	101	J15	Z	149	J15	Z			
16	D17	X	102	J15	Z	150	J15	101*			
20	D17	X	103	J15	101*	151	J15	101*			
27	C4	52	104	J15	Z	152	J15	101*			
30	C4	52	105	J15	101*	153	J15	Z			
31	C4	52	106	J15	Z	154	J15	Z			
32	C4	52	107	J15	Z	156	J15	Z			
33	F6	2	108	J15	Z	157	J15	101*			
34	F6	2	109	J15	101*	158	J15	Z			
35	F6	2	110	J15	Z	159	J15	Z			
36	F6	2	111	J15	101*	160	J15	Z			
37	C7	2	114	J15	Z	161	J15	101*			
38	C7	2	116	J15	101*	162	J15	101*			
41	F6	2	118	J15	Z	163	J15	Z			
42	F6	2	119	J15	101*	164	J15	Z			
44	D19	U	120	J15	Z	166	J15	Z			
52	D17	X	121	J15	101*	167	J15	101*			
54	D17	X	122	J15	Z	168	J15	Z			
55	D17	X	123	J15	Z	170	J15	Z			
56	D17	X	124	J15	Z	171	J15	Z			
57	D17	52*	125	J15	101*	172	J15	101*			
58	D17	52*	126	J15	Z	174	J15	Z			
59	D17	52*	127	J15	Z	175	J15	Z			
60	D14	Z	128	J15	Z	176	J15	101*			
61	D14	Z	130	J15	Z	179	J15	Z			
62	D14	Z	131	J15	101*	181	J15	Z			
63	D14	60*	132	J15	Z	182	J15	Z			
64	D14	Z	133	J15	101*	183	J15	Z			

* Boiler Pressure 150 lb. † Cylinders 10″ × 18″.

21

184	J15	101*	251	J9	N	322	D2	W
185	J15	Z	252	J9	N	323	D2	W
186	J15	Z	253	J15	101*	327	D2	W
187	J15	101*	254	J15	Z	328	D2	W
188	J15	Z	255	J15	Z	329	D2	W
190	J15	101*	256	J15	Z	330	D2	W
191	J15	101*	257	J4	N	331	D2	W
192	J15	101*	258	J4	N	332	D2	W
193	J15	Z	259	J4	N	333	D4	O
194	J15	Z	260	J4	257	334	D4	O
195	J15	101*	261	J4	N	335	D4	O
196	J15	101*	262	J4	N	336	D4	O
197	J15	Z	263	J4	N	337	D4	O
198	J15	Z	264	J4	N	338	D3	O
199	J15	Z	269	C5	•S	339	D4	O
200	J15	Z	270	C5	S	340	D4	O
201	J11	101	271	C5†	S	342	D4	O§
202	J11	60	274	C5	S	343	D4	O§
204	J12	60	276	G3	276	344	D4‖	O
207	J11	101	279	E1	S	345	D4	O§
208	J11	60	290	G3	276	346	D4‖	O
209	J11	101	291	G3	276	351	J9	N
210	J11	60	293	G3	276	352	J9	257
211	J3	351	295	E2	S	354	J9	N
212	J3	351	296	D15‡	276	356	K3	Q
213	I1	351	298	D15	276	357	K3	Q
214	I1	351	299	J28	299	358	K3	Q
217	J11	101	301	D11	N	359	K3	Q
218	J11	60	302	D11	N	360	K3	Q
219	J11	101	303	D11	N	361	K3	Q
220	J11	60	304	D11	N	369	K4	Q
222	J25	276	305	D12	O	370	K4	Q
223	J15	101*	306	D12	O	372	K1	D
229	J15	101*	307	D12	O	373	K1	D
232	J15	101*	309	D10	N	374	K1	D
234	J17	276	310	D10	N	375	K1	D
236	J17	276	311	D10	N	376	K1	D
237	J17	276	312	D10	N	377	K1	D
239	J17	276	313	D10	N	378	K1	D
240	J15	101*	314	D10	N	379	K1	D
241	J15	101*	317	C7	2	380	K1	D
242	J15	101*	318	C7	2	381	K1	D
243	J15	101*	319	C7	2	382	K1	D
249	J9	N	320	C7	2	383	K1	D
250	J9	N	321	D2	W	384	K1	D

* Boiler Pressure 150 lb.   ‡ Cylinders 16½" diameter.
† Cylinders 15¾" diameter.   § Boiler Pressure 160 lb.
‖ Cylinders 17" diameter.   Pressure 175 lb.

385	K1	D	460	C3	458	574	J18	X
386	K1	D	461	K2	N†	575	J18	X
387	K1	D	462	K2	461	576	J18	X
388	K1	D	463	B4	R	582	J18	X
389	K1	D	464	B4	R	583	J18	X
390	K1	D	466	B4	R	584	J18	X
391	K1	D	467	B4	R	585	J18	573‡
393	K1a	D	468	B4	R	586	J18	573‡
394	K1a	D	470	B4	463	587	J18	X
395	K1a	D	495	M3	495	588	J18	X
396	K1a	D	500	B1	400	589	J18	X
397	K1a	D	501	B1	400	590	J18	X
398	K1a	D	502	B1	400	591	J18	X
401	B2a	K	530	D16§	X	592	J18	573‡
402	B2a	K	532	D16	530‡	593	J18	573‡
403	B2	K	533	D16	530‡	594	J19	573‡
405	B2	K	534	D16	X	595	J19	X
406	B2a	400	535	D16	530‡	596	J19	X
407	B2	400	536	D7	C	597	J19	X
409	B2	400	537	D7	C	598	J19	X
423	G1	267	538	D7	C	599	J19	X
424	G1	T	539	D7	C	600	J19	594‡
425	G1	T	540	D6	C	601	J19	X
428	F2	T	541	D6	C	602	J19	X
430	F2	T	542	D6	C	603	J19	X
431	F2	267	543	D6	C	604	J19	X
432	F2	T	544	D6	C	605	J19	X
433	F2	267	545	D5	A	606	J19	X
434	F1	101	546	D5	A	607	J19	X
435	F1	101	547	D5	A	608	J19	X
436	F1	101	548	D5	A	609	J19	X
437	F1	101	550	D5	A	610	J19	X
438	F1	101	551	J26	E	612	J19	573
439	F1	434	552	J26	E	613	J19	X
443	J8	351	553	J26	E	614	J10	573
444	J8*	442	554	J26	E	615	J10	573
445	J8	351	555	J26	E	616	J10	573
446	J8	451	556	J26	E	617	J10	594
448	J1	448	557	J26	E	618	J10	573
454	D8	451	558	J26	E	619	J6	H
455	C2	351	559	J26	E	620	J6	H
456	C2	351	560	J26	E	621	J6	H
457	C2	351	561	J26	E	623	J5	C
458	C3	458	562	J26	E	624	J5	C
459	C3	458	567	J16	X	625	J5	C

* Wheels 4′ 11½″ diameter.   ‡ Boiler Pressure 150 lb.

† Boiler Pressure 160 lb.   § Cylinders 15½″ diameter.

23

626	J5	C	655	G2	Y	711	J15b	Z
627	J5	C	656	G2	650*	712	J15b	Z
628	J5	C	657	G2	650*	713	J15b	Z
629	J5	C	658	G2	650*	714	J15b	Z
630	J5	C	659	G2	650*	715	J15b	Z
631	J5	C	660	G2	Y	716	J15b	Z
632	J5	C	661	G2	Y	717	J15b	Z
633	J5	C	662	G2	650*	718	J15b	Z
634	J5	C	663	G2	Y	719	J15b	Z
635	J5	C	664	G2	650*	800	B1a	M
636	J5	C	665	G2	650*	801	B1a	M
637	J5	C	666	G2	650*	802	B1a	M
638	J5	C	667	G2	Y	850	P1	850
639	J5	C	668	G2	Y	1000	J1a	
640	J5	C	670	I3	Z	1001	J1a	
641	J5	C	671	I3	Z	1002	J1a	
642	J5	C	672	I3	Z	1003	J1a	
643	J5	C	673	I3	Z	1004	J1a	
644	J5	C	674	I3	Z			
645	J5	C	700	J15a	700	Argadeen	K5	
650	G2	Y	701	J15a	700	St. Molaga	L6	
651	G2	Y	702	J15a	700	Jumbo	J13	
652	G2	Y	703	J15a	700	Sambo	L2	
653	G2	Y	704	J15a	700			
654	G2	Y	710	J15b	Z			

* Boiler Pressure 150 lb.

Narrow Gauge (3 ft.)

Numbers and Classes

1C	BN4		1L	DN2		4S	DN5	
2C	PN1		2L	DN2		6S	EN1	
3C	BN3		3L	DN2		1T	KN2	
5C	IN1		4L	DN2		2T	KN2	
6C	IN1		8L	DN2		3T	KN2	
7C	BN3		10L	FN1		4T	KN1	
9C	PN1		12L	FN1		5T	PN2	
10C	BN1		13L	FN1		6T	KN2	
11C	BN2		3S	DN4		8T	KN2	

Named Engines

800	Maedhbh		802	Tailte		1L	Isabel
801	Macha					3S	Kent

C.I.E. AND CONSTITUENT COMPANIES

Locomotive Superintendents and Chief Mechanical Engineers

G.S.W.R.

1845	J. Dewrance
1847	G. Miller
1864	A. MacDonnell
1883	J. A. F. Aspinall
1886	H. A. Ivatt
1896	R. Coey
1911	R. E. L. Maunsell
1913	E. A. Watson
1922	J. R. Bazin

M.G.W.R.

1847	J. Dewrance
1849	(contractor)
1853	C. E. Wilson
1856	J. Cabry
1862	R. Ramage
1872	M. Atock
1901	E. Cusack
1915	W. H. Morton

D.S.E.R.

1854	W. Pemberton
1856	S. W. Haughton
1864	W. Meikle
1865	J. Wakefield
1882	W. Wakefield
1894	T. Grierson
1897	R. Cronin
1917	G. H. Wild

G.S.R. & C.I.E.

1925	J. R. Bazin
1929	W. H. Morton
1932	A. W. Harty
1937	E. C. Bredin
1942	M. J. Ginnetty
1944	C. F. Tyndall

PRINCIPAL LOCOMOTIVE SHEDS

G.S. & W. Section	...	Inchicore, Maryborough, Thurles, Limerick Junction, Mallow, Cork, Limerick, Tralee, Waterford, Rosslare.
M.G.W. Section	...	Broadstone, Mullingar, Athlone, Galway, Westport, Sligo.
D.S.E. Section	...	Grand Canal Street, Bray, Wexford.
C.B.S.C. Section	...	Cork (Albert Quay).
C. & L. Section	...	Ballinamore.
W.C. Section	...	Ennis.
W. & T. Section	...	Waterford (Manor).

PRINCIPAL DIMENSIONS OF C.I.E.

LOCOMOTIVES

Class	Wheels	Designer	Building Date	Cyls.	Driving Wheels	Boiler Pressure	Weight of Loco (t. cwt.)	Tractive Effort
B1	4-6-0	Bazin	1924-26	19½"×28"	6' 7"	180	73 02	23,780
B1a	,,	Bredin	1939-40 (3)	18½"×28"	6' 7"	225	84 00	33,000
B2	,,	Watson/Morton	1921	19½"×26"	6' 7"	180	75 10	19,150
B2a	,,	Watson/Bazin	1921	19½"×28"	6' 7"	180	75 10	20,620
B4	4-6-0T	Beyer Peacock	1906-20	18"×24"	5' 2½"	160	55 04	16,920
C2	4-4-2T	Cronin	1911-24	18"×26"	6' 0"	160	64 16	15,912
C3	,,	Sharp Stewart	1893	18"×26"	5' 3"	160	57 17	17,050
C4	,,	Coey	1900	17"×22"	5' 8½"	150	54 13	11,830
C5	,,	Robinson*	1896-97	16"×24"	5' 6"	150	50 12	11,870
C6	,,	Ivatt	1894-02	16"×20"	5' 8½"	150	50 11	9,530
D2	4-4-0	Coey	1904-06	18"×26"	6' 7"	180	55 06	16,315
D3	,,	Coey	1908	17"×26"	5' 8½"	180	52 10	16,780
D4	,,	Coey/Harty	1907-36	18"×26"	5' 8½"	180	51 10	18,800
D5	,,	Cusack	1902-05	18"×26"	6' 3"	175	52 00	16,700
D6	,,	Cusack	1909-15	18"×26"	6' 3"	175	50 00	16,700
D7	,,	Cusack	1909-12	18"×26"	6' 3"	175	49 00	16,700
D8	,,	Cronin	1905	18"×26"	6' 1"	160	45 19	15,700
D10	,,	Coey	1903	18"×26"	6' 7"	160	48 04	14,500
D11	,,	Coey	1900	18"×26"	6' 7"	160	47 00	14,500
D12	,,	Coey	1902	18"×26"	6' 7"	180	49 16	16,315
D14	,,	Aspinall	1885-95	18"×24"	6' 7"	160	41 00	13,390
D15	,,	Robinson*	1896	17"×24"	6' 0"	150	40 16	12,280
D16	,,	Atock	1900-01	16"×22"	5' 8"	160	40 10	11,260
D17	,,	Aspinall	1883-90	17"×22"	6' 7"	160	39 01	10,920
D19	,,	McDonnell	1877-80	16"×20"	5' 8½"	150	34 10	9,530
E1	0-4-4T	Avonside	1876	17"×24"	5' 3"	150	49 19	14,040
E2	,,	Kitson	1895	16"×24"	5' 6"	150	43 00	11,870
F1	2-4-2T	Cronin	1901-09	17"×24"	5' 6"	150	52 10	13,400
F2	,,	Wakefield/Cronin	1886-98	17"×24"	5' 6"	150	50 10	13,400
F6	,,	Ivatt	1892-4	16"×20"	5' 8½"	150	46 04	9,530
G1	2-4-0T	Wakefield	1885-96	17"×24"	5' 6"	150	41 13	13,400
G2	2-4-0	Atock	1893-8	17"×24"	5' 8"	160	37 10	13,870
G3	,,	Dubs	1889-94	17"×24"	6' 0"	150	38 11	12,280
I1	0-6-2T	Coey	1903	18"×26"	4' 6½"	160	57 11	21,020
I3	,,	Harty	1933	18"×26"	5' 6"	160	57 11	16,025
J1a	0-6-0	Diesel Electric	1947-48	487 h.p.	4' 0"		52 19	24,000
J1	,,	Kitson	1897	18"×26"	4' 9"	160	46 15	20,090
J3	,,	Coey	1903	18"×26"	4' 6½"	160	44 00	21,020
J4	,,	Coey	1913-14	19"×26"	5' 1¾"	160	46 11	20,670
J5	,,	Morton	1921-24	19"×26"	5' 8"	175	47 11	20,530
J6	,,	Avonside	1878	18"×24"	4' 9"	175	45 12	20,290
J8	,,	Cronin	1904-10	18"×26"	5' 1"	160	42 07	18,780
J9	,,	Coey	1903-12	18"×26"	5' 1¾"	160	46 12	18,560

* J. G. Robinson, Loco. Supt. W.L.W.R., 1888-1900, afterwards C.M.E., Great Central Railway (England)

PRINCIPAL DIMENSIONS OF C.I.E.

LOCOMOTIVES—continued

Class	Wheels	Designer	Building Date	Cyls.	Driving Wheels	Boiler Pressure	Weight of Loco	Tractive Effort
							t. cwt.	
J10	0-6-0T	Atock	1881-90	18″×24″	4′ 6″	150	44 19	18,360
J11	,,	Ivatt	1887-01	18″×24″	4′ 6½″	150	40 04	18,200
J12	,,	McDonnell	1879	18″×24″	4′ 6½″	150	45 13	18,200
J13	,,	McDonnell	1876	18″×24″	4′ 6½″	150	37 03	18,200
J15	0 6 0	McDonnell	1866-03	18″×24″	5′ 1¾″	160	37 13	17,170
J15a	,,	Bazin	1929	18″×24″	5′ 1¾″	160	41 00	17,170
J15b	,,	Harty	1934	18″×24″	5′ 1¾″	160	43 00	17,170
J16	,,	Atock	1880	18″×24″	5′ 1¾″	160	40 09	17,195
J17	,,	Robinson*	1901	18″×24″	5′ 2″	150	41 04	15,990
J18	,,	Atock	1876-95	18″×24″	5′ 3″	160	38 10	16,785
J19	,,	Atock	1885-89	18″×24″	5′ 3″	160	39 00	16,785
J25	,,	Robinson*	1895-00	17″×24″	5′ 2″	150	39 16	14,270
J26	0-6-0T	Atock	1891-93	15″×22″	4′ 6″	150	33 12	11,690
J28	,,	Hunslet	1894	12″×18″	3′ 1″	130	23 00	7,460
J30	,,	McDonnell	1875-90	12″×18″	3′ 8½″	150	22 09	7,425
K1	2-6-0	Maunsell	1925-29	19″×28″	5′ 6″	200	62 04	26,040
K1a	,,	Maunsell	1930	19″×28″	6′ 0″	200	62 11	23,870
K2	,,	Wild	1922	19″×26″	5′ 1″	175	50 01	22,800
K3	,,	Coey	1903	19″×26″	5′ 1¾″	180	57 02	23,260
K4	,,	Coey	1909	19″×26″	5′ 1¾″	180	57 02	23,260
K5	2-6-0T	Hunslet	1894	14″×18″	3′ 6″	145	28 00	10,350
L2	0-4-2T	Maunsell	1913	16″×20″	4′ 6½″	150	34 13	11,980
L6	,,	Hunslet	1890	10½″×16″	3′ 3″	145	21 17	5,575
M3	0-4-0T	Peckett	1920	10″×15″	2′ 9″	160	18 00	6,180
P1	2-6-2T	Bazin	1928	17½″×28″	5′ 6″	160	71 10	17,700

NARROW GAUGE

Class	Wheels	Designer	Building Date	Cyls.	Driving Wheels	Boiler Pressure	Weight of Loco	Tractive Effort
BN1	4-6-0T	Carter	1903	15″×20″	3′ 0″	150	39 00	15,940
BN2	,,	Carter	1909	15″×20″	3′ 6″	150	36 00	13,660
BN3	,,	Carter	1922	15″×20″	3′ 9″	150	39 10	12,750
BN4	,,	Carter	1912	15″×20″	3′ 9″	150	40 00	12,750
DN2	4-4-0T	Stephenson	1887	14″×20″	3′ 6″	150	26 00	11,900
DN4	,,	Peckett	1914	12″×18″	3′ 0½″	150	24 10	9,660
DN5	,,	Nasmyth Wilson	1888	12″×18″	3′ 4″	150	24 00	8,260
EN1	0-4-4T	T. Green	1893	14″×20″	3′ 6″	145	25 00	11,500
FN1	2-4-2T	Neilson	1899	14½″×22″	4′ 6″	150	39 00	10,920
IN1	0-6-2T	Hopkins	1892	15″×20″	3′ 6″	150	35 12	13,660
KN1	2-6-0T	Kerr Stuart	1903	12½″×20″	3′ 0″	160	36 00	11,805
KN2	,,	Kerr Stuart	1889-10	13″×18″	3′ 0″	150	38 10	10,770
PN1	2-6-2T	Hopkins	1898-00	15″×20″	3′ 6″	150	38 00	13,660
PN2	,,	Hunslet	1892	13½″×18″	3′ 0″	150	39 10	11,620

* See footnote, p. 26.

THE RAILWAYS OF IRELAND

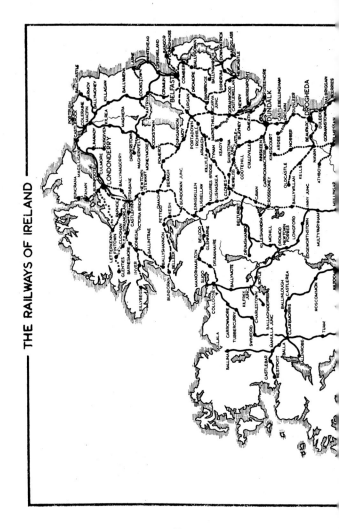

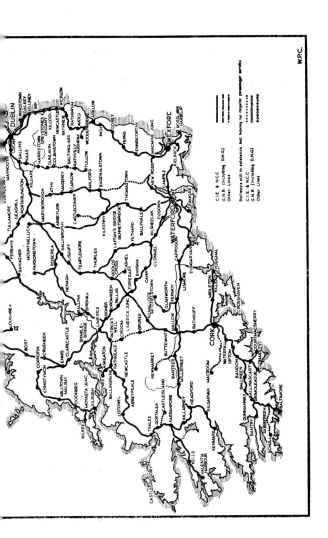

W.P.C.

Railways still in existence but having no regular passenger service

C.I.E. & N.C.C.
G.N.R. (including D.N.G.)
Other Lines

C.I.E. & N.C.C.
G.N.R. (including D.N.G.)
Other Lines

Great Northern Railway

The Great Northern Railway (Ireland) came into being only on 1st April, 1876, after four important companies decided to amalgamate under that name. These were the Ulster Railway, the Dublin and Drogheda, the Dublin and Belfast Junction and the Irish North Western. The oldest of these was the Ulster Railway, connecting Belfast with Armagh through Portadown, where it exchanged traffic with the Dublin and Belfast Junction Railway. The Ulster Railway was first opened for traffic in August 1839, with the section from Belfast to Lisburn. By 1852 there was rail communication between Belfast and Dublin, with the exception of a gap over the River Boyne at Drogheda. Passengers had to travel by road from the Belfast Junction Station situated on the Northern bank of the River, to the Dublin and Drogheda station, which had been erected close to the site of the present station. With the aid of a loan from the British Treasury a viaduct and bridge were constructed so as to complete the existing gap.

On 5th April, 1855, the newly constructed section was opened for traffic, though through working between Dublin and Belfast had been possible by means of a temporary bridge since 22nd June, 1853.

In 1929 the question of rebuilding this bridge came to the front. The line was double throughout, so the cost of reconstruction was high. After many plans had been drawn up it was found that the structure could be strengthened at lesser cost by interlacing the tracks. This plan was approved and in 1930 work was commenced and within two years the bridge had been renovated.

One of the most interesting features about the G.N.R. (I) is the fact that it operates in two countries, and crosses frontiers. The fact that Customs formalities exist has a detrimental effect upon the time-keeping of trains. Moreover Customs stations are to be found, not only at Dundalk and Goraghwood on the main line between Dublin and Belfast, but also on the Irish North Western Section from Dundalk to Enniskillen as well as between Strabane and Londonderry.

The main line of the G.N.R. is well adapted for fast running. From Dublin to Dundalk gradients are relatively easy except for the 4 miles rise at 1 in 177 from Drogheda to Kellystown Box, and the subsequent descent of $7\frac{1}{2}$ miles mainly at 1 in 197. The stiffest rise takes place after Dundalk where the line winds its way through the mountains to Goraghwood with gradients of 1 in 100.

At present the timings of the express trains are not so fast as in 1939, but owing to necessary repairs to tracks and consequent slacks, it has been considered inexpedient to press forward with accelerated timings. Reference must be made to the non-stop "Enterprise" express which runs between Belfast and Dublin. It was introduced in August, 1947, the 112½ miles taking 2¼ hours, giving an average running speed of 50 m.p.h. On 31st May, 1948, a second "Enterprise" express was introduced from Dublin to Belfast and return, the timings being the same as for the earlier express.

The peak of express services on the G.N.R. was in 1932, when the compound engines were first introduced. The time-tables included a nonstop run from Dublin to Dundalk in 54 minutes for the 54¼ miles and a number of bookings over the 31¾ miles between Dublin and Drogheda in 33 minutes down and 32 minutes up : there were bookings of 2 hours 20 minutes between Dublin and Belfast, inclusive of three stops and customs examination, the running time allowed for the 112½ miles being only 122 minutes. The necessity for economy after the prolonged strike of 1933 led to the easing of these timings, though very fast running continued until the war.

Generally speaking the stock of the G.N.R. is rather more recent than many of the locomotives and vehicles of C.I.E., and they are more fully standardised.

The G.N.R., which operates 827½ miles of track (including sidings), is ⅃ concern which well repays study. It is well administered, and the timing enthusiast can find excellent work performed by all classes of engines.

G.N.R. LOCOMOTIVES

The G.N.R. when formed in 1876 had naturally an enormous variety of locomotives, but after the appointment of J. C. Park as Locomotive Superintendent in 1880 a process of standardisation began which has continued since with the progressive elimination of the older types, so the present locomotive stock can be described briefly.

Park first built 4-2-2 engines (long scrapped) and his first 4-4-0 express engines, now class P 6 ft. 6 in., did not appear till 1892. They proved rather too small and Clifford, in 1895, produced the PP class with larger cylinders and firebox, which continued to be built for lines with restricted axle loads till 1911. The Q class of 1899 were similar, but larger all round, and these were followed in 1904 by the QL class with still larger boilers. Finally the S class of 1913 continued the same basic design, but with superheaters and piston valves ; in these engines, however, as only 17 tons per axle was then permitted, it was necessary to revert to a smaller boiler, similar in diameter to the Q class, but longer and with much larger firebox.

From 1920 on, Mr. Glover rebuilt all the older types with superheater boilers. The Q class were first dealt with and were given

8 in. piston valves above the cylinders, but in order to avoid the use of rocking arms and the necessity for raising the boiler centre line, advantage was taken of the 5 ft. 3 in. gauge to give the QL, PP and P classes 6½ in. piston valves placed *between* the cylinders.

The S class had their pressure raised from 175 to 200 lbs. about 1926, and in 1938-9 they were completely renewed with long travel valves. Some of the work performed by this class, in both original and rebuilt states, was very remarkable for engines of their limited size.

In 1932 Mr. Glover had produced the only engines on the line which were a definite departure from the Park-Clifford tradition, the five 3-cylinder compound V class engines. These had originally 250 lbs. pressure ; the effect of their introduction on the time-tables has already been referred to, but when the trains were slowed their pressure was reduced.

The year 1947 saw the first Belpaire boilers on the G.N.R., used for rebuilding the compounds, and Mr. McIntosh's new engines are generally similar to the Belpaire compounds except for the adoption of three simple cylinders. For branch lines there have always been four-coupled engines with smaller driving wheels ; Park's first type of 5 ft. 7 in. 4-4-0 have long disappeared, but the small wheeled version of the P class are still in service : in 1915 Mr. Glover introduced a new type, with superheater and piston valves, and driving wheels increased to 5 ft. 9 in., the U class, of which five modernised examples were added by Mr. McIntosh in 1948.

Of passenger tank engines there are only two classes. The JT class 2-4-2T are a tank version of the old 2-4-0 branch line tender engines long scrapped and the class T 4-4-2T exactly correspond to the U class tender engines.

The goods engines also have always been built in series corresponding to the contemporary passenger engines. Class A corresponded to the small 2-4-0s and Class AL to Class P 5 ft. 6 in. After this the same class letter was used for both passenger and goods engines, with the addition of G to the goods engines. Classes PG and QG have been superheated with slide valves, QLG and QNG with piston valves. With the appearance of the SG class in 1913 the standard driving wheel for goods engines was increased from 4 ft. 7¼ in. to 5 ft. 1 in. diameter, and in 1921 an enlarged version of the SG class was built, SG3, with larger boilers and cylinders, which has no passenger counterpart. These are the largest 0-6-0 engines in Ireland. The goods version of the U class did not appear until 20 years after the passenger engines, and a further five improved engines were added in 1948. These are mixed traffic rather than goods engines.

Of the goods tank engines, class QGT correspond to the QG class, but class R are deceptive engines, being built for the restricted loading gauge of some of the Belfast dock lines. In spite of their

relatively massive appearance, they are only the equivalent of the
A class engines.

Finally a word about the only 4-4-0T, No. 195, which has for
many years been the Dundalk shunting engine. This is now the last
non-standard engine, having come from the Belfast Central Railway,
which was absorbed by the G.N.R. in 1885. The last engines dating
from before the amalgamation of 1876, three Irish North Western
and one Ulster, were withdrawn in 1948.

Considerable use is made of Diesel railcars, the earlier designs
being for branch lines, while the later ones are for the Dublin and
Belfast suburban services, and where the traffic is insufficient even
for Diesel railcars, converted road buses fitted with Howden-
Meredith patent wheels are used.

DIESEL RAILCARS

Index Letter	Horse Power	Weight t. c.	Total Seats	See Note
A	102	19 00	48	1
C1	102	14 05	50	2
C2	102	15 00	48	2
C3	102	15 00	46	2
D	153	39 10	159	3
E	153	39 10	159	3
F	204	41 05	164	4
G	204	41 05	164	4

NOTES :
1. Single unit car.
2. Engine on separate unit articulated to body : cars C2 and C3 normally work
   back to back as a double unit.
3. Double unit articulated to six-coupled central power bogie.
4. Double unit articulated to four-wheel central power bogie with individual
   drive.

DIESEL RAIL BUSES

No.	H.P.	Weight	Seats
1	62	6 t. 00 c.	31
2	62	6 t. 00 c.	28
3	62	6 t. 00 c.	28
4	62	6 t. 00 c.	30

G.N.R.

NUMERICAL LIST OF ENGINES WITH CLASSES

1	T2	46	PP	91	JT	135	Q
2	T2	47	SG3	92	JT	136	Q
3	T2	48	SG3	93	JT	139	T2
4	T2	49	SG3	94	JT	140	AL
5	T2	50	PP	95	JT	141	AL
6	SG3	51	P 5′ 6″	96	SG3	142	T2
7	SG3	52	P 5′ 6″	97	SG3	143	T2
8	SG3	53	P 5′ 6″	98	QGTs	144	T2
9	QLG	54	P 5′ 6″	99	QGTs	145	UG
10	PG	55	AL	100	PG	146	UG
11	PG	56	AL	101	PG	147	UG
12	PP	57	AL	102	PG	148	UG
13	SG3	58	AL	103	PG	149	UG
14	SG3	59	AL	104	P 5′ 6″	150	A
15	SG2	60	A	105	P 5′ 6″	151	PG
16	SG2	62	T2	106	PP	152	QG
17	SG2	63	T2	107	PP	153	QG
18	SG2	64	T2	108	QLG	154	QG
19	SG2	65	T2	109	QLG	155	QG
20	SG3	66	T2	110	QLG	156	QL
21	T2	67	T2	111	QLG	157	QL
22	RT	69	T2	112	QNG	158	QLG
23	RT	70	PP	113	QL	159	QLG
24	QL	71	PP	115	T2	160	QLG
25	P 6′ 6″	72	P 6′ 6″	116	T2	161	QLG
26	P 6′ 6″	73	P 6′ 6″	117	SG3	162	QLG
27	P 6′ 6″	74	PP	118	SG3	163	QLG
28	A	75	PP	119	QLG	164	QLG
29	AL	76	PP	120	Q	165	QLG
30	T2	77	PP	121	Q	166	RT
31	Crane	78	UG	122	Q	167	RT
32	AL	79	UG	123	Q	168	QGT2
33	AL	80	UG	124	Q	169	QGT2
35	AL	81	UG	125	Q	*170	S
36	AL	82	UG	126	QL	*171	S
38	QNG	*83	V	127	QL	*172	S
39	QNG	*84	V	128	QL	*173	S
40	SG3	*85	V	129	PP†	*174	S
41	SG3	*86	V	130	Q	175	SG
42	PP	*87	V	131	Q	176	SG
43	PP	88	P 5′ 6″	132	Q	177	SG
44	PP	89	P 5′ 6″	133	Q	178	SG
45	PP	90	JT	134	Q	179	SG

* Named Engines　　　　　† 4′ 3″ boiler, weight 42 tons 12 cwt.

180	SG2	188	T1	198	U	*206	VS
181	SG2	189	T1	199	U	*207	VS
182	SG2	*190	S2	200	U	*208	VS
183	SG2	*191	S2	*201	U	*209	VS
184	SG2	*192	S2	*202	U	*210	VS
185	T1	195	BT	*203	U		
186	T1	196	U	*204	U		
187	T1	197	U	*205	U		

*Named engines

Named Engines

83	Eagle	173	Galtee More	204	Antrim
84	Falcon	174	Carrantuohill	205	Down
85	Merlin	190	Lugnaquilla	206	Liffey
86	Peregrine	191	Croagh Patrick	207	Boyne
87	Kestrel	192	Slievenamon	208	Lagan
170	Errigal	201	Meath	209	Foyle
171	Slieve Gullion	202	Louth	210	Erne
172	Slieve Donard	203	Armagh		

G.N.R. PRINCIPAL RUNNING SHEDS

Dublin	Derry	Belfast (Adelaide)
Drogheda	Newry	Clones
Dundalk	Portadown	Enniskillen

G.N.R. Locomotive Superintendents and Chief Mechanical Engineers

1881	J. C. Park	1933	G. B. Howden
1895	Charles Clifford	1939	H. R. McIntosh
1912	G. T. Glover		

PRINCIPAL DIMENSIONS OF G.N.R. ENGINES

Class	*Wheels*	*Designer*	*Building Date*	*Cyls.*	*Driving Wheels*	*Boiler Pressure*	*Weight of Loco*	*Tractive Effort*
							t. c.	
A	0-6-0	J. C. Park	1882-91	17"×24"	4' 7¼"	165	34 06	17,686
AL	0-6-0	J. C. Park	1893-96	17"×24"	4' 7¼"	175	38 11	18,758
BT	4-4-0T	Beyer Peacock	1880	16"×20"	5' 0"	165	42 06	11,968
JT	2-4-2T	C. Clifford	1895-02	16"×22"	5' 7"	175	46 02	12,504
P 6' 6"	4-4-0	J. C. Park	1892-95	18"×24"	6' 7"	175	44 08	14,641
P 5' 6"	4-4-0	J. C. Park	1892-06	18"×24"	5' 7"	175	42 02	17,264
PG	0-6-0	C. Clifford	1899-04	17½"×24"	4' 7¼"	175	39 14	19,879
PP	4-4-0	C. Clifford	1896-11	18"×24"	6' 7"	175	45 09	14,641
Q	4-4-0	C. Clifford	1899-04	18½"×26"	6' 7"	175	49 04	16,755
QG	0-6-0	C. Clifford	1903-04	17¾"×26"	4' 7¼"	175	42 16	22,054
QL	4-4-0	C. Clifford	1904-10	18½"×26"	6' 7"	175	49 19	16,755
QLG	0-6-0	C. Clifford	1906-11	19"×26"	4' 7¼"	175	49 02	25,385
QNG	0-6-0	C. Clifford	1911	19"×26"	4' 7¼"	175	47 12	25,385
QGTs	0-6-2T	C. Clifford	1905	18½"×26"	4' 7¼"	175	55 06	24,080
QGT2	0-6-2T	C. Clifford	1911	18½"×26"	4' 7¼"	175	60 00	24,080
RT	0-6-4T	C. Clifford	1908-11	17"×24"	4' 3"	165	56 00	18,074
S, S2	4-4-0	C. Clifford	1913-15	19"×26"	6' 7"	200	53 06	20,198
SG, SG2	0-6-0	C. Clifford	1913-24	19"×26"	5' 1"	175	48 19	22,887
SG3	0-6-0	G. T. Glover	1920-21	19½"×26"	5' 1"	175	52 10	24,107
T1	4-4-2T	G. T. Glover	1913	18"×24"	5' 9"	175	65 04	16,763
T2	4-4-2T	G. T. Glover	1921-29	18"×24"	5' 9"	175	65 15†	16,763
U	4-4-0	G. T. Glover	1915	18"×24"	5' 9"	175	44 06	16,763
U	4-4-0	H. McIntosh	1948	18"×24"	5' 9"	200	46 00	19,158
UG	0-6-0	H. McIntosh	1937-48	18"×24"	5' 1"	200	45 12*	21,671
V	4-4-0	G. T. Glover	1932	(HP) 17¼"×26" (LP) 19"×26"	6' 7"	215	65 01	20,435
VS	4-4-0	H. McIntosh	1948	(3) 15¼"×26"	6' 7"	220	66 06	21,462
Crane	0-6-0T	Hawthorn Leslie	1928	14"×20"	3' 4"	200	45 00	16,660

*** Nos. 145-149 (built 1948) weigh 46 tons 17 cwt.**

† Some engines have boiler pressure 200 lbs., tractive effort 19,158 lb.

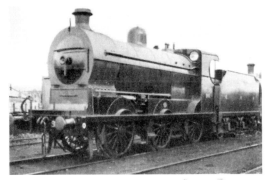

Top : No. 96,
Class SG3

Right : No. 169,
Class QLG,
fitted for oil
burning, being
refuelled at
Dublin

[Photos: J. M. Robbins

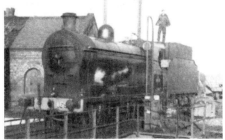

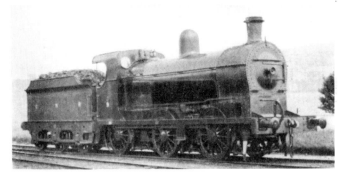

No. 9, Class QLG

[H. C. Casserley

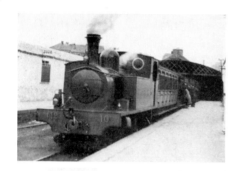

L. & L.S.R.

4-6-2T No. 10 on Buncrana train in Londonderry Terminus

H. C. Casserley

G.N.R.

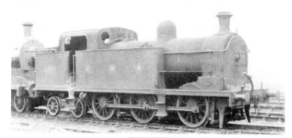

Above : Class RT 0-6-4T No. 167

[*H. C. Casserley*

Right : G.N. Diesel Rail-bus, No. 1

Below : Twin Diesel Railcar, F

[*Photos: R. N. Clements*

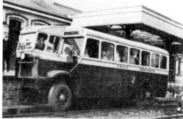

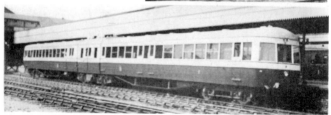

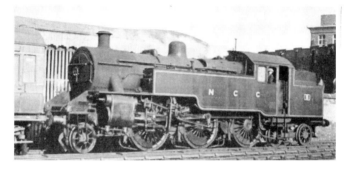

2-6-4T Class WT
No. 5

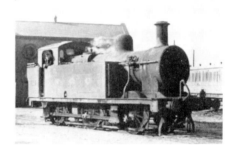

Right : 0-6-0T, Class
Y, No. 18, formerly
L.M.S. No. 7456

[*Photos: H. C. Casserley*

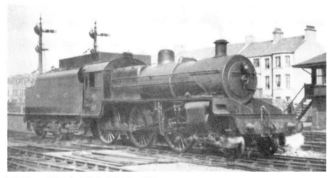

W Class " Mogul " 2-6-0 No. 102   [*J. M. Robbins*

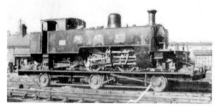

Narrow gauge compound 2-4-2T No. 42 on
5′ 3′ gauge transporter truck

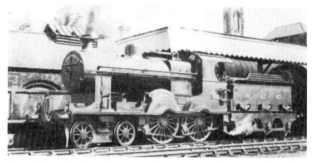

Class B3 4-4-0 No. 60 *County Donegal*, a well-known class that
became extinct while this ABC was in preparation

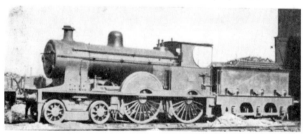

[Photos: H. C. Casserley

Class D1 4-4-0 No. 50 *Jubilee*, withdrawn.　The class has been
extinct since since 1946

Northern Counties Committee

The Northern Counties Committee, formerly owned by the L.M.S.R., is now attached to the London Midland Region of the British Railways, though it is probable that this will be only a temporary arrangement. It serves the Northern part of the Six Counties, connecting Belfast with the towns of Londonderry, Coleraine, Portrush, Ballymena and Larne. The mail route from Northern Ireland to England passes through Larne, there being a night service in each direction, augmented by one during the day, operative in the summer months.

As early as 1836 a proposal was brought forward to establish a railway between Belfast and Ballymena, but the scheme was abandoned owing to the financial depression. Eight years later the project was revived and in April 1848 the line was opened. In 1860 the bridge over the River Bann, at Coleraine, was completed, and permitted a through service of trains between Belfast and Londonderry. It is interesting that the Belfast & Northern Counties Company, as it was then known, introduced third class travel by all trains as early as 1862, a change which was not applied in England until many years later. In 1903 the B. & N.C.R. was purchased by the Midland Railway and the name changed to "Midland Railway (Northern Counties Committee)." In 1923 another change was made to L.M.S.R. (N.C.C.). The most recent change in name has followed the nationalisation of railways in Great Britain, and this concern is now known as "The Railway Executive (N.C.C.)."

During the period of its existence the N.C.C. has acquired three 3 ft. 0 in. light railways, namely, the Ballymena and Larne Harbour, the Ballymena-Parkmore (Retreat) and the Ballycastle, as well as the Londonderry and Strabane. Only the last two are working normal traffic. The Ballymena and Retreat was the first to be taken up in 1937, while in 1940 the section from Ballymena to Ballyboley was closed. Trains now run occasionally from Larne to the paper mills at Ballyclare.

Until the year 1934 all trains travelling to the main line had to reverse at Greenisland Junction, but in that year the Greenisland Loop and viaduct were opened, so that all trains could travel direct and omit the stop at Greenisland. A few trains continue to run direct from the Larne to the main line over the old track, but since the loop has been opened this section has been reduced to single track. During the war there was a daily passenger train in either direction running between Londonderry and Larne Harbour, as well as troop and leave trains, one of which was for the G.N.R. (I) travelling via Antrim and Lisburn.

In 1943, during the late war, an R.A.F. aerodrome was constructed at Ballykelly between Limavady Junction and Londonderry.

The runway for the planes had to be extended across the railway tracks, and a special signalling installation was brought into use for the safety of both trains and aeroplanes.

On leaving Belfast the gradients are stiff out to Ballyclare Junction on the main line and Greenisland on the line to Larne. The rise from Whiteabbey (4.3 miles) to Mossley (7.0 miles) is at 1 in 76½. The summit is at Kingsbog Junction (9.1 miles), after which the line falls steadily to Antrim at inclinations of 1 in 178,186. Approaching Ballymoney there is a 5½ miles descent with gradients as steep as 1 in 97 (though this is short), but the general incline is about 1 in 120.

The main line is double throughout from Belfast to Ballymena, after which it is single. Automatic staff exchange has been installed, so that it is possible for staffs to be exchanged at speeds as high as 60 m.p.h. and over. At passing places the track has been straightened out to permit fast travelling. On the Larne line the track is double as far as Whitehead.

The peak of fast travel took place in 1939, when a timing of 60 m.p.h. was in operation between Ballymena and Belfast, the 31 miles being timed in 31 minutes. On the Larne line, the boat express in either direction was allowed 30 minutes for the 24.3 miles, an excellent timing, as part of the line is single.

During April and May 1941 two severe air raids on Belfast took place. Much serious damage was done to the railway ; in the first raid the General Stores Dept. and Parcels offices were destroyed ; during the second raid even more extensive damage was caused, including the Station Hotel, inwards and outwards goods store, as well as twenty coaches and 250 wagons destroyed or seriously damaged.

The N.C.C. controls 346½ miles of track, including sidings. Jointly with the G.N.R. (I) it owns the County Donegal Joint Committee, though a separate manager, at Stranorlar, supervises this narrow gauge concern on behalf of the two companies.

N.C.C. LOCOMOTIVES

The revolution which has taken place in the locomotive stock of the N.C.C. during the past 15 years is shown by the fact that of 28 classes in use in 1932 only 7 survive now ; and of the 36 locomotives running in 1932 which are still in service, no fewer than 27 belong to classes A1 and U2.

These (except for No. 4A) are the only remaining four-coupled tender engines, and of the popular 0-6-0 type only three are left ; the only other tender engines are the now ubiquitous 2-6-0s of Class W, a design derived from the L.M.S. 2-6-4T type, but with 6 ft. driving wheels. The 2-6-4T of class WT also differ from their L.M.S. prototypes in this respect.

The few classes mentioned account for the entire broad gauge stock, except for shunting engines and Diesels. No. 16 of class N is used for the Belfast dock lines, and the two engines of class Y were transferred from the L.M.S.R. in 1944. Of the Diesels, No. 28 was running on the B.C.D.R. from 1937 to 1944.

From 1890 to 1908 all new engines built for the B.N.C.R. and N.C.C. were of the two-cylinder compound type, and the four narrow-gauge engines are of very great interest as being the last of these compounds. After the abandonment of the compound principle for the broad gauge it was retained for the narrow gauge, as the last two compound 2-4-2T were built in 1919-20 and were identical with the original engines of 1892.

N.C.C.—ENGINE NUMBERS, NAMES, CLASSES

No.	Class	Name		No.	Class	Name
1	WT			73	U2	
2	WT			74	U2	Dunluce Castle
3	WT			75	U2	Antrim Castle
4	WT			76	U2	Olderfleet Castle
5	WT			77	U2	
6	WT			78	U2	Chichester Castle
7	WT			79	U2	Kenbaan Castle
8	WT			80	U2	Dunseverick Castle
9	WT			81	U2	Carrickfergus Castle
10	WT			82	U2	Dunananie Castle
13	V			83	U2	Carra Castle
14	V			84	U2	Lissanoure Castle
15	V			85	U2	
16	N			86	U2	
17	X			87	U2	Queen Alexandra
18	Y			90	W	Duke of Abercorn
19	Y			91	W	The Bush
22	*			92	W	The Bann
28	*			93	W	The Foyle
33	A1	Binevenagh		94	W	The Maine
34	A1	Knocklayd		95	W	The Braid
41	S1			96	W	Silver Jubilee
42	S1			97	W	The Earl of Ulster
43	S			98	W	King Edward VIII
58	A1			99	W	King George VI
62	A1	Slemish		100	W	Queen Elizabeth
64	A1	Trostan		101	W	
65	A1	Knockagh		102	W	
66	A1	Ben Madigan		103	W	Thomas Somerset
69	A1	Slieve Bane		104	W	
70	U2			111	S	
71	U2	Glenarm Castle		4A	U1	Glenariff
72	U2					

* These locos are on hire from the makers, Messrs. Harland & Wolff and have no class letter.

PRINCIPAL DIMENSIONS OF N.C.C. LOCOMOTIVES

Class	Type	Date	Cylinders	D.W.	B.P.	Weight	Tractive Effort
						t. c.	
A1	4-4-0	1901-08	18″ × 24″	6′ 0″	160	46 07	14,688
N	0-4-0ST	1914	16″ × 22″	4′ 0½″	130	31 01	12,707
S*	2-4-2T	1892-20	14¾″ × 20″ / 21″ × 20″	3′ 9″	160	31 17	13,150
S1*	2-4-2T	1908-09	14¾″ × 20″ / 21″ × 20″	3′ 9″	160	33 00	13,150
U1	4-4-0	1931	18″ × 24″	6′ 0″	170	50 14	15,606
U2	4-4-0	1914-36	19″ × 24″	6′ 0″	170	51 10	17,388
V	0-6-0	1923	19″ × 24″	5′ 2½″	170	47 15	20,031
W	2-6-0	1933-42	19″ × 26″	6′ 0″	200	62 10	22,160
WT	2-6-4T	1946-47	19″ × 26″	6′ 0″	200	87 10	22,160
Y	0-6-0T	1927-28	18″ × 26″	4′ 7″	160	49 10	20,830
X	0-6-0	1936	330 b.h.p. Diesel Mechanical			49 00	24,000
22	0-6-0	1934	225 b.h.p. Diesel Mechanical			27 03	15,000
28	2-2-2-2	1937	500 b.h.p. Diesel Electric			48 00	10,000

* Two-cylinder compound narrow gauge engines.

DIESEL RAILCARS

No.	Power	Length	Seats
1	Two 130 h.p. Leyland Diesel engines.	54 ft.	62
2		60 ft.	82
3		60 ft.	80
4		60 ft.	80

RUNNING SHEDS

Belfast (York Road) | Coleraine | Larne
Ballymena | Derry

County Donegal Railways Joint Committee

The first railway in County Donegal was the Finn Valley Railway from Strabane to Stranorlar, opened on the 5 ft. 3 in. gauge in 1863. In 1882 the West Donegal Railway was built, a 3 ft. 0 in. gauge line from Stranorlar to Donegal, the W.D.R. and the F.V.R. being under the same management. In 1892 the two companies amalgamated as the Donegal Railway, and two years later the broad gauge section was converted to narrow gauge. From that time forward other branches were opened, the last being the Strabane and Letterkenny line in 1909.

In 1906 the Donegal Railway Company was dissolved, the concern being taken over jointly by the G.N.R. and the N.C.C. These two companies, being responsible for expenditure, appointed a manager resident at Stranorlar to supervise the undertaking. The line from Derry to Strabane became the sole property of the N.C.C., although it has always been worked by locomotives and stock of the Joint Committee.

As time elapsed, passenger receipts began to decline owing to road competition. But before the road services became highly developed, Mr. Henry Forbes, the Manager of the Joint Committee, introduced a number of railcars, at first petrol and later Diesel. By so doing he was able to improve and extend the services. Journey times were reduced, and these vehicles were able to stop at level crossings to set down or pick up passengers. Thus an example was set to other railways, as the Company more than held its own with passenger traffic. At present a most reasonable service is in operation, considering the sparseness of the population.

On 13th December, 1947, the branch from Stranorlar to Glenties was closed for all regular traffic, this being catered for by road services provided by the G.N.R. The branch is, however, still utilised for through trains conveying livestock or turf. The Tribunal reporting on this decided that no actual economy would be effected by the change, which was authorised only because the Joint Committee had no means of raising the large sum necessary for renovation of the permanent way.

The County Donegal Railway passes through some of the loveliest scenery in Ireland, through Barnesmore Gap and round Donegal Bay to Killybegs.

C.D.R.J.C. LOCOMOTIVES

The late Henry Forbes, who was Manager of line from 1910 till his death in 1943, was a pioneer in the introduction of Diesel traction to railway work, and practically the entire passenger service, with the exception of the Strabane-Derry section, is worked by Diesel railcars.

This has permitted the steam locomotive stock to be reduced from 21 to 11 engines, all of which are superheated, being the only superheated narrow-gauge engines in Ireland.

The engines are painted geranium red ; coaches and railcars have red lower and cream upper panels.

The works and principal running shed are at Stranorlar.

C.D.R.J.C.
LOCOMOTIVE STOCK

No.	Name		Class	No.	Name		Class
1	Alice	...	5a	8	Foyle	...	5
2	Blanche	...	5a	9	Eske ...	...	4
3	Lydia	...	5a	10	Owenea	...	4
4	Meenglas	...	5	11	Erne ...	...	4
5	Drumboe	...	5	11*	Phoenix	...	*
6	Columbkille...		5	12	Mourne	...	4

* Numbered 11 in railcar series. Bought from Clogher Valley Railway 1932.
Originally an Atkinson Walker steam tractor, converted to Diesel engine 1933.
Gardner 6L2 engine, 74 h.p., four wheels 2' 4" dia., weight 12 tons.

PRINCIPAL DIMENSIONS OF C.D.R.J.C. LOCOMOTIVES

Class	Wheels	Date	Cyls.	D.W.	B.P.	Weight	T.E.
						t. c.	
4	4-6-4T	1904	15" × 21"	3' 9"	160	44 10	14,280
5	2-6-4T	1907-8	14" × 21"	4' 0"	175	43 10	12,755
5a	2-6-4T	1912	15½" × 21"	4' 0"	160	50 08	14,295

RAILCAR STOCK

No.	Total Seats	H.P.	Engine	Chassis
7	30	74	Gardner 6L2	Sixwheel
8	30	74	Gardner 6L2	Sixwheel
10	28	74	Gardner 6L2	Bogie
12	41	74	Gardner 6L2	Bogie
14	41	74	Gardner 6L2	Bogie
15	41	74	Gardner 6L2	Bogie
16	41	96	Gardner 6LW	Bogie
17	43	96	Gardner 6LW	Bogie
18	43	96	Gardner 6LW	Bogie

No. 7 was the first Diesel rail vehicle in the British Isles. All the bogie railcars
are of articulated type, and the four wheels of the power bogie are coupled.

RUNNING SHEDS

Letterkenny   Killybegs   Strabane
Stranorlar (Railcars)   Donegal

Sligo, Leitrim & Northern Counties Railway

The Company owns 43¼ miles of line from Enniskillen to Carrignagat Junction with running powers over 5 miles of the C.I.E. thence to Sligo. It has the peculiarity that its engines, which are painted black have never been numbered, being distinguished by names only.

The works are situated at Manorhamilton : there are two small engine sheds at Enniskillen, but in Sligo the C.I.E. shed is used.

Name				Type	Class
Fermanagh	...	...	...		
Lurganboy	...	...	...	0-6-4T	Leitrim
Hazlewood	...	...	...		
Lissadell	...	...	...		
Sir Henry	...	...	...		
Enniskillen	...	...	...	0-6-4T	Sir Henry
Lough Gill	...	...	...		
Glencar ...	...	...	...	0-6-0	Glencar
Sligo	...	...	...		

PRINCIPAL DIMENSIONS OF S.L.N.C.R. LOCOMOTIVES

Class	Type	Designer	Date	Cyls.	D.W.	B.P.	Weight t. c.	T.E.
Leitrim	0-6-4T	Beyer Peacock	1882-99	16½″×20″	4′ 9″	160	47 10	12,513
Sir Henry	0-6-4T	Beyer Peacock	1904-17	17″×24″	4′ 8″	160	53 10	16,840
Glencar	0-6-0	Chas. Clifford	1882-90	17″×24″	4′ 7″	160	34 06	17,140

Glencar and *Sligo* bought from G.N.R. G.N.R. Nos. 31 and 69.

Railcar

No. B. Gardner 6LW engine ... ... 102 b.h.p. 59 seats

Railbuses

No. A. Gardner 4LW engine ... ... 68 b.h.p. 29 seats
No. 2A. Gardner 4LW engine ... ... 68 b.h.p. 32 seats

Londonderry & Lough Swilly Railway

This Company at one time operated 99 miles of line : the last passenger service (Derry-Buncrana) was withdrawn on September 6th, 1948, though excursions are occasionally run. Goods trains run from Derry to Buncrana and Letterkenny and there are extensive road services : the Company also has four motor vessels in service on Lough Swilly.

Nos. 5 and 6 are the largest narrow-gauge engines in the British Isles, and No. 12 (together with a similar engine No. 11, now scrapped) the only narrow-gauge tender engine which ever worked in Ireland. Since the withdrawal of the G.S.R. 900 class these are also the only eight-coupled engines in Ireland.

The engines are painted bright green, lined yellow.

The works and sheds are at Derry (Pennyburn).

No.	Type	Builder	Date	Cyls.	D.W.	B.P.	Weight	T.E.
							t.	
2	4-6-0T	A. Barclay ...	1902	14″ × 20″	3′ 6″	150	30	11,900
3	4-6-0T	A. Barclay ...	1902	14″ × 20″	3′ 6″	150	30	11,900
4	4-6-0T	A. Barclay ...	1902	14″ × 20″	3′ 6″	150	30	11,900
5	4-8-4T	Hudswell Clarke ...	1912	16″ × 20″	3′ 9″	180	51	17,400
6	4-8-4T	Hudswell Clarke ..	1912	16″ × 20″	3′ 9″	180	51	17,400
8	4-6-2T	Hudswell Clarke ..	1901	15″ × 22″	3′ 9″	150	41	14,050
10	4-6-2T	Kerr Stuart ..	1904	14″ × 20″	3′ 6″	150	35	11,900
12	4-8-0	Hudswell Clarke ...	1905	15½″ × 22″	3′ 9″	170	37	17,160
15	4-6-2T	Hudswell Clarke ...	1899	15″ × 22″	3′ 9″	150	41	14,050
16	4-6-2T	Hudswell Clarke	1899	15″ × 22″	3′ 9″	150	41	14,050

Dundalk, Newry Greenore Railway

The D.N.G.R., though the property of the L.M.S.R. (now of the British Railways) has since 1933 been operated by the G.N.R. Both engines and coaches are of L.N.W.R. design and still retain the old L.N.W.R. livery, but much of the traffic is now worked by G.N.R. engines and coaches.

No.	Name	Wheels	Building Date	Cyls.	Driving Wheels	Pressure	Weight	T.E.
							t. c.	
1	Macrory ...							
2	Greenore ...							
3	Dundalk ...	0-6-0ST	1873-98	17″ × 24″	5′ 2½″	140	35 5	13,026
4	Newry ...							
6	Holyhead ...							

D.N.G.R.

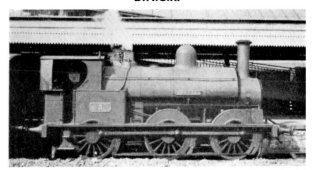

0-6-0T No. 3 *Dundalk*

H. C. Casserley

C.D.R.J.C.

Class 5 2-6-4T
No. 8 *Foyle*

[J. M. Robbins

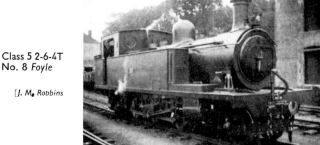

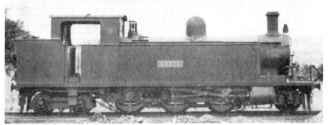

Class 5a 2-6-4T No. 3 *Lydia*

[H. C. Casserley

49

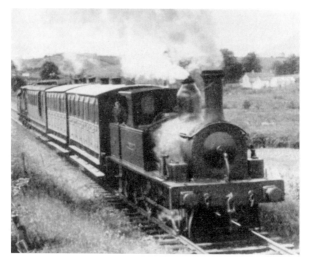

0-6-4T *Lissadell* on train just inside Eire, near Manorhamilton

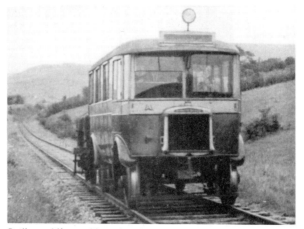

Railbus "A" near Manorhamilton
[*Photos: H. C. Casserley*

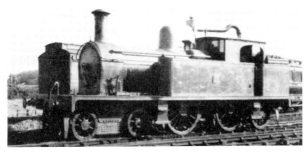

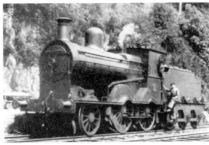

Above : 4-4-2T
No. 30 at New-
castle
[*J. M. Robbins*

Right : 2 - 4 - 0
No. 6
[*R. N. Clements*

Below : ''Baltic''
(4 - 6 - 4T) tank
No. 23 at Belfast
[*J. M. Robbins*

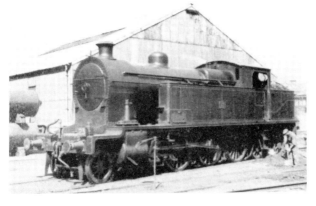

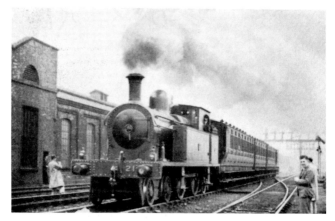

Leaving Belfast, 4-4-2T No. 21 and a four-coach train

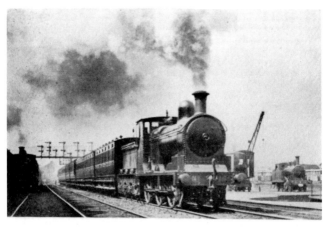

0-6-0 No. 14 heading a train out of Belfast

[*Photos : H. C. Casserley*]

Belfast and County Down Railway

This railway operates exclusively in County Down, its main line being from Belfast to Castlewellan, a distance of 41½ miles. The oldest portion of the system is from Belfast to Holywood, which was opened for traffic in 1848, being subsequently extended to Bangor by another company, which was acquired by the B.C.D.R. in 1884. The main line to Downpatrick was opened in 1859, but it was not until 10 years later that there was any rail connection with Newcastle.

On October 1st, 1948, the B.C.D.R. was taken over by the Ulster Transport Authority, which now controls both rail and road transport in the six counties.

In 1861 a project was set on foot for a mail packet service to operate between Donaghadee and Portpatrick. Great efforts were made to bring this about, the British Treasury undertaking to finance part of the scheme. Work was pushed forward, alterations were made to the harbours at both places and the line from Newtownards to Donaghadee was constructed, as well as one from Stranraer to Portpatrick on the Scottish side. The scheme, however, fell through.

The B.C.D.R. main line from Belfast is double to Comber, 8 miles, and to Bangor, 12 miles. Over the single line to Newcastle automatic staff exchange apparatus has been installed, as there are a few semi-fast trains. Prior to the last war a " Golfers' Express " used to run all the year round on Saturdays between Belfast and Newcastle, and in summer on the early closing day in the former city. The time allowed was 50 minutes for the non-stop journey of 37.1 miles.

Although fast trains are few, yet the work performed by the standard 4-4-2 tanks is very smart, as the gradients are steep and the bookings far from easy : speeds of over 60 m.p.h. have been recorded on the downhill stretches.

It should be mentioned that traffic operation has been undertaken by the G.N.R. on behalf of the directorate of this Company, and similarly all the engineering side is supervised by officials of the G.N.R. There is a connecting line from the B.C.D.R. to the G.N.R., known as the Belfast Central, which is valuable for the interchange of traffic, and over this portion of railway it is possible for wagons to be transported to and from the quays on both sides of the River Lagan. Since the G.N.R. has undertaken the traffic control of the B.C.D.R., the goods station at Queen's Quay has been closed, all traffic now being dealt with at the Grosvenor Road G.N.R. depot.

Road competition has seriously affected traffic on this railway, the distance from Belfast to nearly all stations except those on the Bangor branch being shorter by road. But the residential traffic on the Bangor branch is heavy, with a frequent service of trains throughout the day.

B.C.D.R. LOCOMOTIVES

Only one passenger tender engine remains, No. 6. This is the last of four 2-4-0 engines of which the other three were two-cylinder compound engines of the same design as used by the Belfast & Northern Counties Railway, and No. 6 was built as a simple engine for comparison. The B.C.D.R. was not so successful with compounds as the B.N.C.R. Some compound tank engines were converted to simple after only a few years and the three 2-4-0s were withdrawn in 1921. No. 6 would have met the same fate ere now were it not for the locomotive shortage due to increased traffic during the war; instead, as new engines were unobtainable, she was rebuilt with a boiler similar to that of the standard 4-4-2T.

No. 28, the 0-4-2T (No. 9 till 1945), which is the oldest engine on the line, is one of a class of 0-4-2 tender engines rebuilt as tanks in the early 1900's, and in this form is the last survivor of the 0-4-2 type, once the most numerous in Ireland. It is also the only engine on the line not built by Beyer-Peacock, who have supplied all new engines since 1891. The three small 2-4-2T are used for the Ballynahinch and Ardglass branches and for motor trains between Belfast and Holywood.

The standard type of 4-4-2T were built from 1901 to 1921, these do practically all the main line work in addition to running to Bangor and Donaghadee; they have been a remarkably successful type and in summer, when loads are heavy, there must be few engines called on to do harder work in proportion to their limited size.

In 1920 the Baltics were introduced for the Bangor line, where the morning and evening trains are heavy and the gradients very severe. Owing to their weight they are not allowed to run elsewhere, so, when new engines were required in 1924, two larger 4-4-2T engines were built, of which the performance is practically equal to that of the Baltics and which can also run to Donaghadee. A third engine of this type was added in 1945.

The goods engines, which are also used frequently on heavy suburban trains, number four. No. 26 is a small engine, but the other three are generally similar, though not identical.

There is now only one Diesel, No. 2, used on the Ardglass or Ballynahinch branch. The other, which was No. 28, is now working on the N.C.C.

All engines, both passenger and goods, are painted dark olive green, lined red and white.

The locomotive works are at Belfast (Queen's Quay) and most of the engines are stationed there.

LOCOMOTIVE NUMBERS AND CLASSES

No.	Class	No.	Class	No.	Class	No.	Class
1	1	9	8	17	1	25	22
2	2	10	4	18	1	26	26
3	1	11	1	19	1	27	5
4	4	12	1	20	1	28	28
5	5	13	1	21	1	29	29
6	6	14	14	22	22	30	1
7	5	15	1	23	22		
8	8	16	8	24	22		

PRINCIPAL DIMENSIONS OF B.C.D.R. LOCOS.

Class	Wheels	Builders	Building Date	Cyls.	Driving Wheels	Pressure	Weight	T.E.
							t. c.	
1	4-4-2T	Beyer Peacock	1901-21	17″×24″	5′ 6″	160	56 18	14.292
4	0-6-0	Beyer Peacock	1914-21	18″×26″	5′ 0″	160	44 00	19,904
5	2-4-2T	Beyer Peacock	1896-97	16″×24″	5′ 6″	160	48 14	12,660
6	2-4-0	Beyer Peacock	1894	17″×24″	6′ 0″	160	37 07	13,101
8	4-4-2T	Beyer Peacock	1924-45	18″×26″	5′ 6″	170	66 00	18,443
14	0-6-0	Beyer Peacock	1904	18″×26″	5′ 0″	160	40 18	19,094
22	4-6-4T	Beyer Peacock	1920	19″×26″	5′ 6″	170	81 12	19,340
26	0-6-0	Beyer Peacock	1892	17″×24″	5′ 0″	160	33 18	15,721
28	0-4-2T	Sharp Stewart	1887	16″×22″	5′ 0″	150	49 10	11,264
29	0-6-4T	Beyer Peacock	1923	17″×24″	4′ 0″	160	55 10	19,584
2	2-4-0	Harland & Wolff	1933	270 h.p. Diesel Electric			33 00	9,450

Industrial Locomotives

ARTHUR GUINNESS & CO. LTD.

The St. James' Gate Brewery, Dublin, is served by 8 miles of 1 ft. 10 in. gauge railway, including a spiral tunnel connecting two different levels on a gradient of 1 in 39. The narrow gauge lines are worked by one Diesel and 19 steam locomotives. The latter are of a very neat type, with cylinders over the boiler and there is an ingenious arrangement by which they can be mounted on broad gauge " haulage wagons " and thus used on the 5 ft. 3 in. gauge. They were designed by Mr. S. Geoghegan, and built from 1882 to 1891, all but No. 6 (Avonside Engine Co.) by the Cork Street Foundry, Dublin.

There are about 2 miles of broad gauge track, and in addition to the narrow gauge engines mounted on haulage wagons, two broad gauge engines built by Hudswell Clarke are in use.

Nos. 2 and 3 are the broad gauge 0-4-0ST engines, with cylinders 15 in. by 22 in., wheels 3 ft. 4 in. diameter, pressure 175 lb., weight empty 24 tons, tractive effort 18,400 lb.

Nos. 6 to 24 are narrow gauge 0-4-0T engines, cylinders 7 in. by 8½ in., wheels 1 ft. 10 in. diameter, pressure 180 lb., weight 7 tons 15 cwt., tractive effort 2,900 lb.

No. 25 is a narrow gauge " Planet " Diesel locomotive by F. C. Hibbert & Co., 1948 ; 37 b.h.p., weight 7 tons, tractive effort 3,500 lb.

COMHLUCHT SIUCRE EIREANN

Twelve shunting locomotives are in use in the four sugar-beet factories.

Nos. 1 to 3 of the Carlow Factory are 0-4-0T built by John Cockerill in 1925. They have cylinders 11$\frac{7}{16}$ in. by 12½ in., wheels 2 ft. 3½ in. diameter, pressure 176 lbs., weight 20 tons, tractive effort 7,400 lbs.

Nos. 1 to 3 of the Thurles, Mallow and Tuam Factories are 0-4-0T by Orenstein & Koppel, 1934. Cylinders 11$\frac{3}{16}$ in. by 15¾ in., wheels 2 ft. 7½ in. diameter, pressure 176 lbs., weight 19 tons 14 cwt., tractive effort 9,800 lbs.

There is also an 80/88 h.p. 4-cylinder Ruston oil shunting locomotive obtained in 1948 for the Carlow Factory.

BRITISH ALUMINIUM CO. (Larne Harbour)

Three 0-4-0T 3 ft. 0 in. gauge engines built by Peckett, 1904, 1906 and 1914. Nos. 1 to 3. Cylinders 7 in. by 10 in., wheels 1 ft. 8 in., pressure 160 lbs., weight 7 tons, tractive effort 3,330 lbs.

LONDONDERRY PORT AND HARBOUR
COMMISSIONERS

Some of the trains on the Commissioners' railway are composed partly of broad and partly of narrow gauge trucks ; the track is gauntletted, and the locomotives are fitted with both combined buffer and drawhook coupling for the narrow gauge and standard three-link coupling for the broad gauge. Both engines are broad gauge. No. 1, 0-6-0ST, was built in 1891 by R. Stephenson & Co., and No. 3, " R.H. Smith," 0-6-0ST, in 1928 by the Avonside Engine Co.

No.	Cylinders	Wheels	Pressure	Weight	T.E.
1	13″ × 18″	3′ 6″	100	23 tons	6,085
3	14″ × 22″	3′ 6″	160	30 tons	13,960